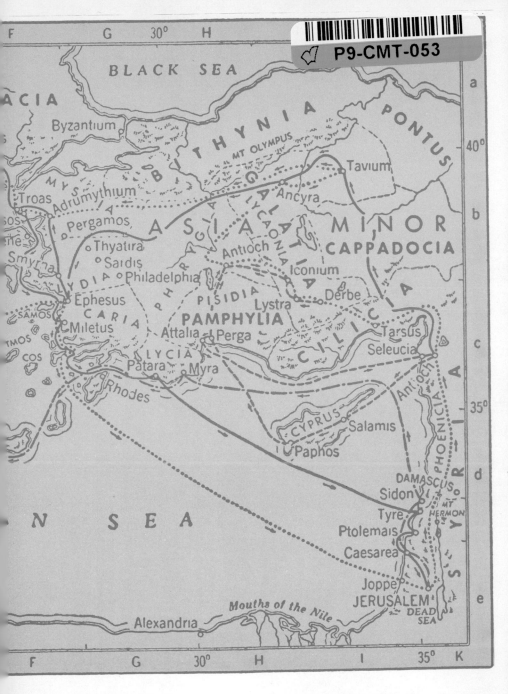

_____ 3rd Journey   _._.._.._Voyage to Rome

ACTS OF
THE APOSTLES
EXPLAINED

ACTS OF THE APOSTLES EXPLAINED

A doctrinal commentary

Prospero
Grech, O.S.A.

alba house - DIVISION OF THE SOCIETY OF ST. PAUL
STATEN ISLAND, N.Y. 10314

Translated by Gregory Carnevale, O.S.A.

This book was first published by Editrice Ponte Nuovo - Bologna, under the title "Atti Degli Apostoli."

Nihil Obstat:
Donald A. Panella, M.A., S.T.L., S.S.L., Censor Deputatus
Imprimatur:
✠ Terence J. Cooke, D.D., V.G.
New York, N.Y. — June 30, 1966

Library of Congress Catalog Number: 66-27531

Designed, printed and bound in the U.S.A. by the Pauline Fathers and Brothers of the Society of St. Paul at Staten Island, New York as a part of their communications apostolate.

CONTENTS

PREFACE

The publication of a new commentary on the Acts of the Apostles requires some justification. To claim that the present volume says anything completely new is utter presumption; its only end is to call the attention of N.T. scholars to some aspects of Acts which have hitherto not received the emphasis they deserve. Luke's second book has been treated too much as a purely historical work while scant attention has been paid to its theology, in particular, to its editorial theology. It is now agreed that the author's purpose was not to write a history of the nascent Church. He selected various episodes from the lives of Peter and Paul and linked them together in a continuous narrative for some doctrinal purpose.

The present commentary is a synthetical work which is meant to be read as a whole. It concentrates on the wood rather than on the trees, leaving the verse-by-verse discussions to other excellent analytical works already in existence. Its purpose is to bring out in as limpid a way as possible the editorial theology of Luke's historico-doctrinal composition.

Among the literature to which I am indebted I wish to signal out J. Dupont's various studies, J. C. O'Neill's *The Theology of Acts* (S.P.C.K., 1961), Conzelmann's latest commentary (*Handbuc zum N.T.*, 1963) and his *Die Mitte der Zeit* (E.T. Faber and Faber 1960), and particularly E. Haenchen's monumental commentary in Mayer's series (1956). Haenchen has done for Acts what Von Rad did for Genesis. Particularly fundamental for the present re-consideration of Acts, then, is H. J. Schoeps' *Theologie und Geschichte des Judenchristentums* (Tübingen 1949). M. D. Goulder's *Type and History in Acts* (S.P.C.K. 1964) came into my hands when the manuscript was already completed and I was glad to see that many of our conclusions overlap, though I am less skeptical than he is about the fundamental historical value of the events narrated by Luke.

The absence of footnotes and bibliography is explained by the fact that I had the general reader in mind, particularly college students, when writing the book. If, however this small commentary renders some modest contribution to Lucan research it will all go to demonstrate how inexhaustible are the riches of the theology of the third Evangelist.

* * * * *

This book was originally written, and partially published, in Italian (*Atti degli Apostoli*, Ed. "Ponte Nuovo," Bologna, 1964). Rev. Gregory Carnevale, O.S.A. translated the manuscript into English.

INTRODUCTION

It is difficult for a Christian living today to imagine the Church composed of a large Hebrew majority with just a scattering of communities converted from paganism. Such, however, was precisely the state of the Church for the first two-hundred years following the death of Christ. The Hebrews had a century-old religious tradition, a doctrine revealed by God, a Law given by Moses on Mt. Sinai, and certain religious mores which were so strong, that they seemed at times to be the very essence of their religion. The pagans, on the contrary, did not even have an exact idea of God; they lived in superstition and vice. Yet, they were accepted as equals to the Jews in the new religion. None of the religious practices which characterized their Palestinian co-religionists were imposed upon them; they were not circumcised, nor did they practice the Mosaic Law or fulfill the rabbinical traditions. The more enlightened Jews of the Christian community adapted themselves to the signs of the times under the promptings of the Holy Spirit; but there were still those who were not able to adjust so easily. Either they opposed any mission to the Gentiles, or, if there had to be such a mission, they demanded that the Gentiles enter the Church by first entering the Synagogue. They would have to be circumcised, observe the Law of Moses and at the same time, be baptized and believe that Jesus was the Lord. This was the mind of the Judaeo-Christian community.

The most ardent opponent of this mentality was the Apostle Paul. He affirmed that if our salvation comes by observing the Mosaic Law, through our own efforts, there would be no need for Christ. How could we say that Christ's death is the source of our justification? Are we not, in fact, reducing to nothing the gift of God? (Gal. 2:21).

Paul's adversaries were not convinced by his arguments and they attacked him strongly, denying him his Apostolic mission and even his right to preach. Besides being attacked by the Christian Jews, Paul was also beset by the non-believing Jews who considered him a traitor and a transgressor of the ancient ancestral traditions. They did not content themselves with only verbal attacks, they threatened him and attempted to take his life. They accused him before the Roman courts of disturbing the peace in various provinces; other Christians were similarly accused by them.

Such accusations were not without their effects. Nero's persecutions revealed that there were not a few anti-Christian sentiments prevalent in the minds of the common people, even though the accusation of the emperor that the Christians were responsible for the burning of Rome was hardly accepted by public opinion. Christians were considered anti-social and promoters of a foreign superstition.

From this environment grew the need to correct such ideas. Needed was a clear-cut explanation of the reason which had led to the evangelization of the Gentiles and also a clarification of the part Paul had played in this mission. Such a mission had actually been begun by Peter, who carried it out not on his own initiative, but rather reluctantly, under the inspiration of the Holy Spirit. Besides, the Church had fully approved of his Apostolic labor. In the last analysis, however, the message of salvation was passed on to the Gentiles mainly on account of the incredulity of the Jews, as had been foretold by the Prophets of old. The Holy Spirit, whose presence among the Gentiles was the sign that they too could receive the Messianic gift, justified the greatest step forward in the early beginnings of the Church.

On the other hand, there arose the need to answer the accusations of the Jews before the Gentiles. The new believers never conspired against the State. In fact, every time they had been brought into court, they were never found guilty of any civil misdemeanor.

This tremendous undertaking was taken up by Luke himself, a Gentile convert from Antioch, a doctor and a travelling companion of St. Paul. According to tradition, and there never has been a weighty reason to make one think otherwise, St. Luke was the author of the third Gospel and of the "Acts of the Apostles" (this title goes back to a manuscript of the middle half of the second century). The style and the theology of the two works are very similar and both show universalist and de-eschatologizing tendencies; i.e., the work of salvation promised by the Prophets for the Messianic era would take place in history before the final coming of the eschatological Kingdom of God and the Parousia of Jesus Christ.

Luke had to choose a form that would aptly carry his thought. Would he write a circular letter or a theological treatise? Our author chose an historical literary style modeled on the historical books of the Old Testament and contemporary Greek works. It must be noted that Luke had no intention of writing a history of the primitive Church, nor a biography of Peter and Paul. Uppermost in his mind was to express a certain theological theme in its historical perspective. That is why he so scupulously collected all the necessary material from various sources either written or oral, adding facts which he himself had personally witnessed (this is seen clearly in passages where he expresses himself in the first person plural). As a result, he felt free to arrange his material in such a way that it gave apt expression to his theological ideas; he cared more for clarity of theological expression than

14

for historical perspective or chronology. Hence the reader, but still more the exegete, must try to discover *why* Luke chose to narrate such a particular episode than *what* he chose to narrate. This does not mean to say that the events narrated are not historical, at least as history was then understood; it only means that Luke was not so much interested in relating the events, as in solidifying the doctrines and tenets of the Church of his time. Following contemporary style and norms, Luke inserted many long discourses into the text (a full 30% of the Acts is devoted to discourses). The framework for such discourses came from tradition, but within this framework he interlaced his own personal ideas, so that he could more aptly present his thought. It is not surprising then that these speeches permeate the style of the entire work. This does not detract from the fact that the discourses of St. Peter in the first chapters help us in a marvelous way to reconstruct the kerygma (the preaching that announced the presence of Messianic salvation to him who believed in Jesus) of the primitive Church.

Luke, then, wished to communicate a thought. But what was this thought? For him the prime reality was an experiencing of the Holy Spirit who manifested himself by means of miracles and charisms. Salvation was to be found wherever the Holy Spirit was, since it was precisely this pouring out of the Holy Spirit on all the believers that had been indicated by the Prophets as a distinctive sign of the Messianic age. The present

15

age, between the Resurrection of Christ and the Parousia (the second coming of the Lord to judge and save the world) is the period of the Spirit, during which the work of salvation is carried on in time by the Church.

Wherever the Spirit is, there is salvation. If, then, the Holy Spirit descended on the community of believers, this was an indication that God had chosen His New People (the community of Christ) in preference to the People of Israel. As the Spirit of God had been active among the Chosen People molding the whole of history around the History of Salvation, so now the Spirit of Jesus operates within the Church guiding its task in the work of redemption.

The Spirit of Jesus directs the expansion of the Church towards Gentile lands. As soon as the pagans believed, they received the Spirit, even before being circumcised. Hence God no longer required the blood of Abraham, the rite of circumcision, or the observance of the Mosaic Law, but only faith in Christ and baptism, through which He called His New People unto Salvation.

The Old Israel, represented by Jerusalem, which "killed the prophets, and stoned those that were sent" (Lk. 13:34), rejected the message of salvation first preached by the Prophets, then by Christ, and finally by the Apostles. Stephen called this attitude "resistance against the Holy Spirit" (Acts 7:51) and Luke himself said: "It is not possible that a prophet perish outside

16

Jerusalem" (Lk. 13:33). Just as in Jerusalem Christ suffered and was delivered up to the Gentiles, so in this same city the Church will be persecuted and the Apostles delivered into the hands of the Romans. The chastisement of Jerusalem came when God withdrew from the Jews this offer of salvation and presented it to the Gentiles, symbolically represented by Rome, the capital of the Hellenistic world. The historical transposition of the Gospel from Jerusalem to Rome symbolized the theological reality of God's temporal abandonment of Israel and His call to the Gentiles.

It is also a sorry fact of history that the Romans persecuted the Church, though the Christians never really did anything to undermine the authority of the State. Before the civil law, primitive Christianity should have enjoyed the same privileges as Judaism, out of which it had originated and of which it was the perfect fulfillment.

Since Acts terminates so abruptly, not mentioning anything about the death of Paul, one might surmise that it was written as soon as Paul was freed from his first imprisonment. This is a weighty argument, but the work breathes the atmosphere of post-Pauline times, around the years 80-90, when the Pastoral Epistles which are very similar in spirit, received their final form. This will appear more clearly in the course of the commentary. The precise date and place of composition still remain a problem to which we have no satisfactory answer.

CHAPTER 1

The Resurrection of Jesus is the foundation of our faith because the Apostles used it as their principal argument to prove that their Master was the Messiah and the Son of God. The faith of the believers was in turn founded on the testimony of those who had seen the Risen Christ with their own eyes and touched Him with their own hands. An Apostle, therefore, was an official witness to the Resurrection of the Lord. To emphasize this, St. Luke tells us that Jesus appeared many times to His disciples as so many arguments to deepen their faith (1:3).

During His life on earth Christ spoke often of the Kingdom of God which He came to found. But in the light of His resurrection, the Kingdom of God took

19

on a new significance. Jesus reinterpreted His teaching in the light of this fact (1:3), promising that the Apostles would, within a short time, receive the Holy Spirit, who constitutes the plenitude of all the Messianic gifts promised by God in the Old Testament (1:4). Pentecost was the beginning of the Kingdom of God in time.

Despite all the explanations given by Jesus about the Kingdom, the Apostles, who still had not received the Spirit, did not yet understand whether the coming of the Kingdom would also imply Christ's immediate return to earth in the Parousia and the restoration of the Kingdom of Israel (1:6). Jesus told them that His final coming would take place in an indefinite future, but before that the Gospel would be preached to Jews, Samaritans, Gentiles and to the whole world (1:8). The chapters that follow will show that the Gospel of the Kingdom, with the assistance of the Holy Spirit, did actually spread from Jerusalem "to the very ends of the world."

v.1. "in the first book"—The Gospel according to Luke. Theophilus—an unknown person.
v.8. Samaria—The Samaritans were Jewish in belief, but of mixed blood; as a result they were considered unorthodox by the Jews.

*   *   *   *   *

20

After the last apparition, Jesus ascended into heaven where He was enthroned at the right hand of the Father. There He received that same glory He had before His Incarnation (Jn. 17:5), which had been hidden during His earthly life. God crowned the work of Jesus, His humility and His obedience unto death on the Cross, raising Him to the dignity that was His due as the Son of God (Phil. 2:7-11). In anticipation of the final coming and total redemption of mankind at the Parousia, God bestowed upon His Son all the supernatural favors that He had prepared for the redeemed human race. These gifts and favors are all contained in the one supreme gift of the Holy Spirit (Acts 2:33).

The clouds which enveloped the Lord (1:9) remind us of the vision of the "Son of Man" of the Prophet Daniel (Dan. 7), an apocalyptic figure who will come to judge the world, with whom Jesus identified Himself (Mt. 25:31f). Thus the angels could proclaim that Christ would return on the last day in the same way as He was taken into heaven.

The Apostles returned to Jerusalem, which, according to Luke, will be the stage on which the drama of salvation history will unfold itself.

v.12. Mount called Olivet—a hill outside of Jerusalem, beyond the Valley of Cedron.

v.13. Upper Room—perhaps the same place as the cenacle where the Last Supper was celebrated.

v.14. The women—those who had been blessed and favored by Jesus and who ministered to Him during His public life (Lk. 8:1-3; 23:49).

v.14. His brothers—since the Hebrew had no word for "cousin," the word "brethren" was used in a wider sense.

* * * * *

Acts 1:15-26 THE ELECTION OF MATTHIAS

One hundred and twenty disciples gathered together, the minimum required by Jewish custom to elect a Sanhedrin. Since the Apostles had to represent both the 12 Tribes of the New Israel and the 12 Judges of the Messianic era, for which the orthodox Jews of today still pray, there was a very definite need to fill the vacancy left by Judas.

In the Acts, St. Peter holds a prominent position among the Apostles, hence the initiative in the election belongs to him, not as a personal whim, but rather as an intuition received from the Scriptures, testifying that the Holy Spirit speaks to the Church through Sacred Writ. The Old Testament, particularly its Messianic texts, was now understood and interpreted in light of the Resurrection of Christ. Before, the Scriptures had spoken to Israel, now they addressed the Church as a living oracle.

Two conditions are required to be an Apostle: (1) to have seen the Risen Lord; (2) and to have received from Him the Divine Mission. Both Barsabbas and Matthias had accompanied Jesus and seen the Risen Lord, but the choice fell upon Matthias who immediately received the apostolic mission, thereby becoming an official witness to the Resurrection of Christ and a member of the ruling elders of the Church.

v.18. Judas—incurred the fate of a sinner described in the Book of Wisdom (4:19).
v.25. "To go to his own place"—in Gehenna, where according to Rabbinical tradition and to Jesus Himself (Lk. 16:23), the souls of sinners went immediately after their death.
v.26. "The Lot"—the ordinary method the pre-exilic Jews employed to determine the will of God. It was done by means of "Urim and Tummin" (cf. e.g., I Sam. 14:41). The Apostles probably used some such method.

* * * * *

CHAPTER 2

Acts 2:1-13 PENTECOST

According to St. John, Jesus bestowed the Holy Spirit upon the Apostles the very day of His Resurrection (Jn. 20:19). However, the Holy Spirit later on often descended upon the believers in a spectacular way (Acts 4:31). The first of these manifestations took place on Pentecost. St. Luke solemnly and dramatically recalls the event to underline the role of the Spirit in the history of salvation.

The Jewish feast of Pentecost, which was celebrated fifty days after the Pasch, was a feast of Thanksgiving for the harvest. In rabbinical writings of the second century after Christ, however, we find the feast celebrated as a commemoration of the day on which God had given the Law to Moses on Mt. Sinai. Since already in the first century Philo of Alexandria had affirmed that the Law came down from heaven like a ball of

25

fire which eventually divided itself into divers tongues destined for all nations, we can suppose that Luke was thinking of this Hebrew tradition and thus presented Pentecost as the bestowal of the "Law of the Spirit" (Rom. 8:1) upon the New Israel and on all nations.

But the theology of Luke really goes much deeper. Just as Jesus began His ministry with the Baptism of the Holy Spirit, so did the Church similarly begin its mission. The Spirit of God had already guided the Chosen People in their most decisive moments; now the Holy Spirit would guide and inspire the destiny of the New People of God. Besides, as St. Peter explains, the Holy Spirit was the gift par excellence promised by the Prophets. The presence of the Holy Spirit clearly demonstrated that the age foretold by the Prophets had finally come and that Jesus was the Messiah. The Spirit bore witness to Jesus (Jn. 15:26) and the experience of the Spirit confirmed the faithful in their faith (Gal. 3:2).

v.2. Mighty wind—the Greek *pnoes* means wind, breath, but symbolically refers to the Holy Spirit.

v.3. Tongues—Luke probably understood the tongues at Pentecost in analogy to the "gift of tongues" with which he was already familiar. The charism consisted in praising God in a language unknown to the speaker himself, but intelligible to his listeners.

26

v.5. They were dwelling in Jerusalem—as pilgrims or residents.

v.9. Parthians, Medes, etc.,—this list comprises all of the then known world, east, west, north and south. Some of the names refer more to ancient biblical times than to the period contemporary to St. Luke: an allusion to the universal salvation foretold by the Prophets.

v.13. Others—a literary technique employed by St. Luke, by which he often divides his audience into two groups: those who sincerely believe and those who stand up and mock the Word of God.

* * * * *

Acts 2:14-40 THE PENTECOSTAL DISCOURSE

In the name of all the Apostles, St. Peter stood up and explained the phenomenon of the gift of tongues, announcing the Resurrection of Christ and demonstrating that Jesus was the Messiah from the recent descent of the Spirit. His argument runs as follows:

"The phenomenon which you are now witnessing is not to be attributed to drunkenness, but to the power of the Holy Spirit. In fact the Prophet Joel had foretold that with the coming of the Messiah, the Spirit, signified by these charismatic gifts, would no longer be given exclusively to the Prophets alone,

27

but would be granted to all the people, even to the most humble. Joel also prophesied that in those days there would be apocalyptic signs portending the coming judgment and that whosoever invoked the name of the Lord would be saved. Consequently, the appearance of the Holy Spirit is an unmistakable proof that we are living in the Messianic era. Remember that Jesus of Nazareth was a man approved by God, as the miracles which He worked testify. Nevertheless you killed Him. God, however, foresaw His death and raised Him up. That Jesus would rise from the dead was foretold even by David the Prophet and we ourselves are living witnesses to the fact that He has truly risen. Jesus is really the Christ. God the Father, raising Him from the dead, enthroned Him at the right hand, conferring on Him all the salvific powers due to the Messiah. Since all the promises of the Prophets are directed to the Messiah, and His People, God gave the Holy Spirit to the Risen Jesus, through Whom this Messianic gift par excellence would be communicated to the People of God. If you wish to receive this pledge of salvation, believe in Christ, do penance and be baptized.

v.15. The Third Hour: About 9 a.m. The Jews did not drink wine in the morning.

v.17. In the last days—the eschatological and final period of salvation history.

28

v.21. The name of the Lord—refers to the Lord Jesus.

v.24. God raised Him up—Christ being God naturally raised Himself to life, but this peculiar expression emphasizes the salvific role of God the Father.

v.33. Having received from the Father the Promise of the Holy Spirit—the Holy Spirit had already descended upon Jesus at His Baptism and accompanied Him during His ministry. However, the Risen and glorified Christ, Who represents the New Israel, received the Holy Spirit in order to communicate It to those who believed in Him.

v.36. Lord—in Greek, *Kyrios,* was the term Hellenistic Jews used for God of Israel; even the pagan Greek gods were called "Lord." The title always referred to some deity. Christ—literally "the Anointed One," the promised eschatological liberator of the Jewish nation. Jesus was the Messiah and Lord from the very instant of His birth, but only after His glorification and because of His obedience unto death did He receive the gift of the Holy Spirit to be communicated to Israel and the nations.

v.38. Repent—*"metanoia"* means a change of heart in relation to God, a realization of one's sinfulness before the Word of God.

v.39. That are far off—the context would seem to indicate the pagans.

* * * * *

In this passage St. Luke describes the life of the first Christians, a life which ought to be the ideal for the Church of every age.

The infant Christian community was still being formed in the environment of mother Israel. The increasing numbers of faithful represented the remnant of faithful Jews standing in the midst of an incredulous people, foretold so often by the Prophets, especially by Isaiah (Is. 7:33 ff). This remnant, chosen by the mercy of God, would carry forward the Gift of God which was rejected by the majority (Rom. 9:27 f).

What was the distinguishing characteristic of this small community? Luke tells us that it was precisely their faith in the Messiah and Baptism (2:41). But the Christians were characterized still more by their lives. They took to heart the good-news of the Apostles (2:42), whose miracles fortified their faith (2:43). They still participated in the common prayer and functions of the temple (2:46; 3:1), but they gradually began to group together by themselves and stand aloof in the Temple (3:11; 5:12). They also had a peculiar liturgy of their own which they were not able to celebrate in the temple. It consisted in the breaking of the Bread, otherwise known as the Eucharist, the rite bequeathed to them by the Lord at the Last Supper. Usually this liturgy was held in private homes, for example, in the house of Mark's mother (12:12).

Communion in the Body of Christ with the Apostles and the whole community tangibly expressed itself in a communal life, a type of life already known to the Essenes of Qumran, and recognized as a high ideal in Judaic society. The Christians, in so far as their numbers would permit them, appropriated this same ideal by selling their possessions and distributing the proceeds to the poor. However, this was just a counsel and not a precept (5:4), which in the form of monasticism has remained in the Church to this day as a symbol of that charity and spiritual communion which ought to inspire the lives of Christians.

Luke also speaks to us about some of the attitudes of the early Christians especially about their awareness of imminent salvation in Christ (2:47) that filled them with a holy fear, but that had filled them above all with an ineffable joy. They praised God continually for the wonderful gift He had given the world in Christ. By their virtuous lives the Christians merited the admiration and praise of all those with whom they came into contact. (2:47).

* * * * *

CHAPTER 3

Acts 3:1-11 THE HEALING OF THE LAME BEGGAR

Isaiah had already prophesied that one of the characteristics of the Messianic era would be that the lame would rise and run like the deer (Is. 35:5 ff). Jesus Himself referred to this prophecy to affirm that He was the promised Messiah (Lk. 7:22). Messianic signs still take place and this time it was Peter who works the miracle—in the name of Jesus. The event attracted the attention of the crowd which was already well disposed towards the Apostles, and at the same time, St. Peter did not lose such an opportune moment to announce the mystery of Jesus.

v.1. The ninth hour: about 3 p.m., the time of the second daily prayer in the temple.

v.2. The Gate of the temple—known as the Beautiful Gate; undoubtedly refers to the principal northeast entrance of the Temple which was also called the Golden Gate or the Corinthian Gate.

33

v.11. The portico called Solomon's—the colonnade on the east side of the Temple where the Christians were wont to meet in prayer.

* * * * *

Acts 3:12-26 THE REIGN OF THE MESSIAH

This discourse of St. Peter surpasses in theological perspective the preceding one of chapter two. The healing of the lame man provided an argument for the existence and the essence of the Messianic era. The argument is somewhat as follows:

> You are eye witnesses of a miraculous healing. It is not we who have worked this miracle by our own virtue or power, but it is God Himself, your God and the God of your Fathers who in a wonderful way effected this miracle to glorify His Son Jesus.

"To glorify" means to reveal the present glory which Christ now has at the right hand of the Father. The allusion to the Canticle of the Servant of Jahweh (Is. 53) recalls the famous prophecy of the passion of the Messiah, the Servant of God (v.13). Peter continues:

> He Whom God has glorified you have killed and therefore you have rejected the Messiah. You did not do this because He was in some way guilty— everyone knows that He was a just man. From the very fact, then, that He suffered, you cannot

34

say that He is not the Messiah. Remember, the Prophets themselves had foretold that the Messiah would suffer. To prove that Jesus is the Messiah, God the Father raised Him up from the dead, and we testify to that fact as eye witnesses. It was He who, through the power of His Son, worked this miracle before your eyes (v.15). What will happen now? Will God punish you? Until now you have acted out of ignorance (v. 17), as Jesus Himself told us from the Cross (Lk. 23:34); perhaps you were ignorant because Jesus was hidden under the veil of the "Messianic Secret." But now God is granting you still another opportunity to be converted, to change your mind about Jesus, to repent of the fact that you denied Him. He is asking you to do penance that your sins may be blotted out. Hardly will you have begun to repent, when God will lead you forth into the "times of refreshing"; then will the promises of the Messianic age be realized when God will send Jesus to you again, the Promised Messiah.

The idea here is similar to that of Romans 1:4, where Paul affirms that Christ "was fore-ordained Son of God by His Resurrection from the dead," which means that the glorified Christ will not have completed His mission until He appears in power and glory as the Son of God to exercise definitively at the final resurrection His salvific mission. Peter continues:

35

Until that day, Jesus will remain in heaven as the Prophet promised by Moses who will be (Deut. 18:15-19) "raised" by God to restore all things (cf. 1 Cor. 15:22-28), and teach us the will of God; He will bless His Holy and Elect People through whom all the nations of the earth will be blessed (v.26; cf. Gen. 12:1-3).

Since the Jews were descendants of the Prophets to whom the original promise was given, they have the right to be blessed first.

The Eschaton will take place when Israel is converted. This was a current rabbinical doctrine, found also in the New Testament (Rom. 11:15; 2 Pet. 3:12). Jesus is the central figure of the eschatological drama which began with His Resurrection. He has blessed the present age, but at the end of time He will exercise the fulness of His mission as Savior (v.20). Jesus began His reign with His glorification and it was through the Holy Spirit that He continued to bless His Kingdom. As such He is the *"Christus revelatus,"* but He has also been chosen to come again on the last day to save and judge the world as the Son of Man of the Prophet Daniel (cf. Acts 7:56—where the Risen Christ is called the "Son of Man"; also in Lk. 22:69). As such Jesus is the *"Christus designatus."*

* * * * *

CHAPTER 4

Acts 4:1-23 THE PERSECUTION OF THE CHURCH

Let us first glance at an outline of the life of Christ according to the Gospel of St. Luke: Christ's Baptism and the theophany of the Holy Spirit, His preaching of the Gospel, His Miracles, His journey to Jerusalem, the persecution by the Jews, His Passion in Jerusalem after having been delivered to the Gentiles, and finally His Resurrection. In the Acts of the Apostles, St. Luke presents the life of the Church in much the same manner: the descent of the Holy Spirit, the preaching of the good-news, miracles and persecution in Jerusalem, all of which point ultimately to a coming Resurrection. Further on we shall see that even the journey up to Jerusalem has a parallel in the Acts. This parallelism was intended by St. Luke, as will be seen from the various passages quoted later on. It suffices now to note the similarity between Acts 4:5-7 and Lk. 22:66 ff: Peter and John are brought before the Sanhedrin in

37

the morning, mention is made of Annas and Caiphas, and questions are put to the Apostles. All this goes to prove that the Church was nothing less than the mystical presence of Christ on earth, a concept which we find also in the letters of St. Paul. The Acts (4:26; 9:4) leaves no room for doubt about this fact.

When St. Luke speaks of "salvation" (v.12) it is that very salvation that Christ came to bring and is symbolized by the healing of the sick.

The blindness of the Jews who persecute the Church as they had persecuted Christ is emphasized all the more by Luke in v.16: "that a notable sign has been performed through them is manifest to all the inhabitants of Jerusalem, and we cannot deny it." Despite this affirmation they remained unbelievers.

v.1. Captain of the Temple—the captain of the police who was on duty in the Temple.

v.2. Resurrection from the dead—the Sadducees, a hellenizing group, associated with the priests and the aristocracy, denied the resurrection from the dead and the existence of angels, both commonly believed by the Pharisees.

v.3. It was already evening—cf. Lk. 22:66.

v.5. Their rulers and Elders and Scribes—these formed the Sanhedrin, the tribunal and the legislative body of the Jews, which comprised seventy-one men chosen from among the High Priests, Pharisees, Sadducees, and doctors of the Law.

v.6. Annas the high priest and Caiphas and John and Alexander—the High Priest at this time was Annas, but his father-in-law, Caiphas, a former High Priest, still wielded great political influence. John and Alexander, forgotten by history, were members of the same family.

v.8. Filled with the Holy Spirit—just as Jesus had promised (Lk. 12:11 ff).

v.11. The stone that was rejected—(Ps. 118 [117]:22), this Psalm, in Jesus' own indication, was one of the texts used by the early Church to show that the Messiah would have been rejected by the Jews (Mt. 21:42; Rom. 9:33; 1 Pet. 2:4).

v.22. He was more than forty years old—with this little description St. Luke underlines the magnitude of the healing of the born cripple.

Acts 4:24-31 BEARING OF THE CHURCH DURING PERSECUTION

Given their liberty, Peter and John returned to find their companions united in prayer and related all that had happened. The reaction of the community to the initial persecutions was neither one of surprise nor alarm. If Christ had suffered it was clear that the Mystical Christ also had to suffer before attaining to final glory. The Passion of the Christ had been foretold in the Scriptures: it was an integral part of the divine plan for the salvation of mankind. Everything the Psalmist says in the second Psalm is equally applicable to the life of the Church.

This Psalm was very popular in the early Church, principally because of v.7, which speaks of the glorification of the Son of God. But in the same context we read of the persecution that the "Anointed One of God" (in Greek, *Christos;* in Hebrew, *Messiah*) would suffer at the hands of kings (Herod), rulers (Pilate), and the people. The Christians applied these words to their own situation, and they prayed not for the cessation of the persecutions, but rather that they should prove to be no obstacle to the preaching of the Gospel. They petitioned the Holy Spirit to continue to render testimony, by miracles and healings, that Jesus was the Messiah.

The answer to their prayer was immediate. As on Pentecost, the Holy Spirit descended upon them, consoling and strengthening them in such a way that miracles were more numerous and the faithful themselves became more holy.

* * * * *

CHAPTER 5

Acts 4:32-5:16 THE HOLY SPIRIT IN THE LIFE OF THE
CHURCH

After relating this second descent of the Holy Spirit
upon the community St. Luke describes the life of
the Christians, a description very similar to that which
follows the feast of Pentecost (2:41-47). He seems
to hint that the union of mind and heart in God is the
effect of the indwelling of the Holy Spirit in the
community.

Luke again mentions that the real reason for this
union in charity was the voluntary action of the community, whereby each one sold his possessions and
distributed the proceeds to the poor, thus putting into
practice what Christ had preached as an ideal (Lk.
12:33f; 18:22). That this was done voluntarily is
clear from the way St. Peter reproved Ananias (5:4),
but those who voluntarily disposed of their goods to

41

contribute to the support of the community were held up as models worthy of imitation. Such a model was Joseph Barnabas who later became the travelling companion of St. Paul.

At this point Satan makes his entrance. He had tempted Christ and consequently he would tempt the Church with some success, as in the case of Ananias and Sapphira (5:3). But he will always be defeated, crushed by the power of the Holy Spirit working through the Apostles (5:3 ff). Even the disciples exorcised, following the example of their Master; this emphasizes the victory of the Church over evil.

The Christians still frequented the Temple and continued to lead holy and edifying lives. The miracles which they worked were also signs of the Messianic era, and they served to glorify and bear witness to Christ. The increasing numbers of the faithful, and the consciousness of their own religious identity gave the sacred writer reason to employ for the first time the word "Church," a word used to describe the infant and growing community. In Matthew 16:18 Jesus had promised to found His own community (quahal= assembly, which refers in particular to the Hebrew assembly at the foot of Mt. Sinai). The word "quahal" is translated into Greek by *"ekklesia,"* thus distinguishing it from *"synagoge,"* which refers to the Hebrew congregations. Here we see the evolution of a consciousness of being a community, a community distinct from the Jews, but at the same time, one directly descended from the ancient People of God. In other words, the community of Jesus, the *Ekklesia*, is the New Israel of the Messianic era.

* * * * *

Acts 5:17-42 THE DIVINE INTERVENTION IN FAVOR OF THE NEW ISRAEL

God had promised Abraham that He would shower blessings on the whole world through Abraham's descendants, the Hebrew people (Gen. 12:1-3). This promise was made in anticipation of the Messiah who was to encompass in Himself the whole People of Israel. Consequently God had guided the history of His People in such a way as to prepare them to receive the Saving Messiah, through Whom they would spread the message of salvation through the whole world.

Christ came. He was crucified by the High Priests but God raised Him up from the dead. Those who believed in Him formed the new offshoot on the aged trunk of Israel, which, because of its incredulity, became displeasing in the sight of God and withered. The history of salvation was to be continued in the New Israel. But the Jews, unaware that God intended salvation to be effected through the Gospel, wished to silence the evangelical message, as they had once tried to silence Christ (cf. Gal. 4:28-31; Rom. 11:7). Their plans were miraculously thwarted by God Who freed the Apostles from prison and providentially defended them against the accusations of the Sanhedrin (Acts 5:19; 26:34). The Apostles for their part accused the Jews of having opposed the plan of God, showing how God had raised up Christ and sent the Holy Spirit (vv.30-32).

The salient point in this chapter is the intervention of Gamaliel in favor of the new religion, moved as he was by a deep feeling of compassion, piety, and good judgment. Time itself, he explained, would determine whether this was the work of God or not. If it is not, then it will die out, just as suddenly as a number of similar movements did a few years before.

St. Luke makes an effort to show that Christain doctrine can be reconciled with Pharisaic Judaism: When Luke wrote the Acts, the Sadducees had already disappeared as a power to be reckoned with. As a result, the Pharisees dominated the entire scene of Judaic theology. Hence we can see why Luke used Gamaliel's plea to summon his contemporaries to re-examine their position in the light of history, especially after the tragic destruction of the temple in 70 A.D.

At this time the infant Church had not yet completely separated itself from Israel. The Apostles were still sounding out every means possible to convert the Jews. Their only response, however, was persistent persecution which led to the final break.

v.34. Gamaliel—probably the son of the famous Hillel. Known mainly because he was St. Paul's teacher,

44

he was also a great doctor of the Law and very moderate in his attitude toward others. He enjoyed a wide reputation and the lasting respect of later generations.

v.36. Theodas—in his famous work *Antiquities of the Jews* (lib. XX c.V.1), Josephus Flavius makes mention of a certain Theodas who travelled the country preaching and causing disturbances. He was finally decapitated by the governor Fado (46-48), roughly ten years after the discourse of Gamaliel.

v.37. Judas the Galilean—immediately after Flavius mentions Theodas, he speaks about the death of Judas the Galilean who died at the time of Quirinus' census in 7 A.D. Since Gamaliel did not know of Flavius' work, it is obvious that Theodas is either another man of the same name and background who has been forgotten by history, or else St. Luke inserted these two figures in the narrative to add the authority of Gamaliel to his argument against the Jews of his time.

* * * * *

CHAPTER 6

Acts 6:1-7 THE COMMUNITY PREPARES ITSELF FOR
HISTORY

The pressure of everyday living forced the community to prepare itself for time and history, a preparation which also took place under the particular guidance of the Holy Spirit.

The intention of St. Luke in this section is not primarily to explain the institution of the diaconate, since the seven are not even called by that name (which is derived from their function of *"diakonia"*= stewardship), but rather Luke intends to accent the contribution made to the Church by the Greeks who introduced their own ideas, as is evident in the preaching of Stephen and Philip.

The Hellenists were the native Jews of the Diaspora, living outside Judea or Galilee; those born in Galilee and Judea were called "Hebrews," and were less prone than the others to universalism. Although the Hellenistic Jews had a deep respect for the Holy City, they nevertheless lived in permanent contact with the pagans, and possessed at the same time a very admirable missionary spirit. Since one of the principal aims of the Acts is to illustrate how the Gospel with the help of the Holy Spirit passed from Jerusalem, through Samaria and the Greek world, to Rome, Luke introduces a select group that would serve to realize this aim.

*   *   *   *   *

CHAPTER 7

The deacon Stephen was the first to suffer physically as His Master had done a short time before, completing what is lacking in Christ's afflictions for the sake of his body (Col. 1:24). We have already seen a definite parallel in the accounts of the Passion of Christ and that of His Church. In this chapter, St. Luke intends another one: Stephen is accused of blasphemy; he is accused of wishing to destroy the Temple; the Scribes stirred up the people and brought false witness against him; "Lord Jesus, receive my spirit" ("Father, into Thy hands I commend my spirit," Lk. 24:48); "Lord, do not lay this sin against them" ("Father, forgive them, for they know not what they do," Lk. 24:34).

This defense of St. Stephen against the Jews is a literary masterpiece. Generally, Luke is very brief, but here he devotes fifty-two verses to the discourse of

49

Stephen. This discourse is not a simple summation of the history of Israel. The accusations against Stephen were already well delineated and stereotyped when the Acts was written. Using Stephen's discourse which was based on tradition, Luke defended the Church against these accusations by arguing on a fundamental theology of history. The new Christian interpretation of the history of Israel came into vogue among the Church Fathers and reached its culmination in the monumental *City of God* of St. Augustine.

Of what was Stephen accused? Had he spoken against Moses, the Temple, God or the Law? He probably preached that Moses and the Law be replaced by Christ and the Gospel, that God had rejected Israel, and that the Temple would be destroyed. Stephen's words are a clarification of this. His theology of history is composed of three basic concepts as beautifully interwoven as a three-part polyphonic motet: (A) God's purpose in giving the land of Israel to the Hebrews had been that they should adore and obey Him; (B) the worship of God is not necessarily restricted to the Temple nor to Israel as a nation. Many theophanies had occurred outside of the promised land, and the Temple itself was of a relatively recent origin; (C) Every time a Prophet was sent by God to the People of Israel, he suffered persecution—the same happened to Moses, Joseph and Jesus. Therefore the Temple will be destroyed as a sign of the Divine reprobation of the People of Israel.

50

Here is the outline of the discourse with the various themes noted in parentheses:

vv. 9-16 Joseph:
Joseph, a man favored by God, was envied by his brothers and was forced to leave his country. God made use of this "persecution" not only to save His People, but also to increase their numbers (C). He will provide for the Christians in a similar manner.

vv. 17-22 Moses was rejected:
The Jews persecuted Moses who was to be their "redeemer, ruler, and judge" and they forced him to flee (C).

vv. 30-34 God was faithful to His promise:
The Lord appeared to Moses on Mt. Sinai, a holy place, even though it was situated *outside* Palestine (B). God, seeing the affliction of His people, sent Moses to save and free them; Moses had taken refuge from them before by fleeing into the desert (C). The parallelism between Moses and the New Moses, Christ, is particularly evident. God first sent Moses when the time of the promise drew near. He was rejected and it was not until after forty years of wandering in the desert that Moses was finally able to free his people. When the time of the Kingdom of God drew near, God sent Jesus; but He also was rejected by the people, and was afterwards taken by God into heaven where He will remain until He comes again to redeem His People once for all.

vv. 35-43 *Application of the Parallelism*:
Moses was rejected in spite of all the "wonders and signs" he worked; but then he was reinstated (v.35/C). This is the thread that leads from Moses to Christ. Jesus is the new Moses, the promised Prophet (Deut. 18:15-18/C). Verse 38 says that Moses was not only the mediator between the Angel (God) and the *"Ekklesia,"* but he was also the spokesman of the word of God to the Church (C). But Moses, rejected while the Israelites adored false gods, called down upon his People the chastisement of God—another veiled threat to Luke's contemporaries.

vv. 43-50 *The Temple was not indispensable*:
When the Israelites were in the desert, God dwelt in the Tent of the Covenant which bore witness against them every time they sinned. This Tent, whose archetype is now in heaven, has no need of an earthly dwelling; even David, who was in a special way favored by God, did not build a Temple (B). This indicates that the Risen Christ is our new Ark of the Covenant and that He bears witness from heaven.

vv. 51-53 *Stephen's conclusion*:
Concluding his recapitulation of the history of Israel, Stephen accused the Jews of consistently opposing the designs of the Holy Spirit, the Hand of God which was always ready to guide the history and faith of the Hebrew People. They resisted the Spirit, persecuted

the Prophets, killed the Messiah and transgressed the Law and the Covenant.

v. 56 *The Son of Man:*
Stephen had a vision of the heavenly Jesus, the Son of Man described by the Prophet Daniel (Dan. 7) and he publicly acknowledged it. The Hebrews "stopped their ears" not wanting to hear such blasphemy, and by so doing they again resisted the Holy Spirit by killing another witness to the Truth.

*   *   *   *   *

CHAPTER 8

Acts 8:1-8 THE DEFINITIVE BREAK WITH THE SYNAGOGUE

The stoning of Stephen was followed by a general persecution of the Church in Jerusalem. The religious and social separation from the synagogue was without doubt complete and the Church finally acquired her independence. God willed that even persecution should serve to spread the Word of the Gospel. The Faithful in Jerusalem were forced to flee to other cities in Judea and Samaria. There with great success they continued to preach the good-news.

The Samaritans held the same beliefs as the Hebrews, but they were of mixed stock and were therefore considered a dissident foreign sect by the Jews. This accounted for the centuries-old enmity between them. The successful preaching of the Gospel by the Deacon Philip in the city of Samaria led the Church one step further from Jewish influence. Had not Jesus

55

so commanded His Apostles to "be my witnesses in Jerusalem and in all Judea and Samaria and to the end of the earth" (Acts 1:8)?

St. Luke slowly works Saul into the narrative picture. He has already been mentioned in passing three times (Acts 7:58, 60; 8:3). It will be Saul, become Paul, who will bring the Gospel to the ends of the then known world.

Acts 8:9-25 SIMON THE MAGICIAN

St. Luke's account of Simon the Magician (from whom derives the word "simony," or the lucrative sale of spiritual goods) is not merely an edifying narration but is in fact a very important part of the whole theological composition of Acts. Simon's teachings were quite widespread in his native country of Samaria in the second century and even penetrated into Rome. His doctrine was a superficial eclecticism with the same Christian elements and pagan beliefs that reflected a nascent gnosticism. Simon himself pretended to be not only the Messiah of the Samaritans, but even God Himself (cf. S. Justin, *Apologia* I, 26 & 56). Without doubt this superstition would have created difficulties for Christian apologists of the second generation. St. Luke here becomes *the* Apologist, demonstrating that Simon fully recognized the power of the Holy Spirit which the Apostles possessed. There were many magicians among the pagans, but the power to effect a miracle was something altogether superior and unique. This power of the Holy Spirit was something that could not be bought, since it was a gratuitous gift of God only to those who believed. Luke proceeds to demonstrate how ridiculous was Simon's request. According to the Sacred Writer, the magician repented of his folly, but in v.24 Simon appears to be inspired more by fear than by a sincere conversion. The exhortation of St. Peter reflects the Church's teaching that even if one sins after Baptism and is repentant, his sins will be forgiven him.

We must also note here that the imposition of hands symbolizes the charismatic communication of the Holy Spirit and does not refer to the internal gift of the Spirit received at Baptism.

v.10. Which is called Great—the "power" of which we read could either refer to the Gnostic doctrine of divine emanation, or the Jewish angelic theology.

* * * * *

Acts 8:26-40 THE TESTIMONY OF ISAIAH

After the account of numerous conversions in Samaria, Luke tells us of another very important conversion, that of the Ethiopian, a minister of Candace the Queen. After his return home the newly converted

Ethiopian undoubtedly preached the "good-news" to his own people. Thus the Kingdom of God continued to spread, guided, of course, by the Holy Spirit. It is obvious, in fact, how the Holy Spirit foreordained everything by sending Philip down to Gaza to meet the eunuch, afterwards "taking him away" when his mission had been completed. The Spirit moved the Apostles at will, much as in a chess game, planning His strategy to capture the world.

The emphasis of this section, however, is mainly on the apologetic value of Isaiah's famous passage about the sufferings of the "Servant of Jahweh." Luke, citing only the 7th and 8th verses of chapter 53, yet including the thought of the entire chapter, speaks of the humiliation of the Suffering Servant, reminding us of the classic passage of St. Paul in his letter to the Philippians (2:6-11). Together with the 22nd Psalm this chapter of Isaiah was the most often quoted of Old Testament passages by the Christian Apologists who proved from Scripture that Christ had to suffer.

Scholars, it is true, dispute at length about the exact identity of the Servant of the Lord in Isaiah. St. Luke, however, does not have the least doubt that it refers to Christ, Who humbled Himself unto death, and whose justice was accepted by God Who raised Him from the dead and glorified Him in heaven, giving Him dominion over all. This was the interpretation St. Luke gave to the Septuagint, even though the Hebrew text has a different version.

v.26. Gaza—a city along the Mediterranean coast on the highway that leads to Egypt.

v.27. Eunuch—he was probably a convert to Judaism and a high official of the court of Candace.

v.27. Candace—not a proper name, but a title used by all the Queens of Meroe and Ethiopia; something similar to the kings of Egypt being called "Pharoa."

v.40. Azotus—Caesarea—two cities along the coast of Palestine, about 18 and 72 miles north of Gaza respectively.

Note: v.27. which is found in some manuscripts possibly reflects an ancient baptismal liturgy.

* * * * *

CHAPTER 9

Acts 9:1-30 THE CONVERSION OF SAUL

The event which we find so dramatically narrated in this chapter is related another two times in Acts (22:3-16; 26:4-18). Why so much emphasis on an event that concerns only a single individual? When Luke wrote this, what did he intend to teach the faithful of his time?

There were probably Jews and Judaizers in Luke's time who doubted by what right the mission to the Gentiles and their admission into the Church had been sanctioned. We know that they often attacked Paul; we read, for example in Gal. 1 and 2 Cor. 3 that as Paul was not one of the twelve he was not considered as an authorized preacher of the Word of God. Since the Acts was specifically intended by Luke to describe and to defend the development of the mission to the Gentiles, the conversion of St. Paul, the Apostle

61

par excellence of the Gentiles, acquired a fundamental importance in the complex theology of the Book. An "Apostle," as we noted above, had to have seen the Risen Christ and had to have received from Him the mission to go and preach the Gospel. This is precisely what happened to St. Paul on the road to Damascus. He beheld the Risen Christ and received from Him the command to go and preach the Gospel to Jews and Gentiles (9:15; 22:14,21; 26:17).

The Sacred Writer's account is the object of rationalistic criticism because of its intrinsic supernaturalism. The liberals wanted to strip the narration of every miraculous aspect and explain it psychologically. Naturally there must have been at least a negative psychological preparation involved in Paul's conversion, but if we discount from the narration God's extraordinary initiative, we would in fact destroy the very fiber of Acts, which was written if for no other reason than to show that the vocation of Paul was a direct act of God Who chose him as His instrument to preach the Gospel to the Gentiles.

This chapter has to be understood in the light of certain events related by Paul himself. His conversion took place in the year 35 or 36, followed by a three year retreat in Nabatea Arabia (Gal. 1:17 f). From Arabia he returned to Damascus which at that time (37-40) was under the dominion of the Nabatean King, Aretas IV (2 Cor. 11:32). Persecuted there by the Jews, Paul fled to Jerusalem (Gal. 1:18) where he met Peter and James. Afterwards he went to his own native city of Tarsus in Cilicia. The first years of his life as a Christian were filled with suspicions on the part of his own brethren in Christ, and with the constant persecutions by the Jews themselves. Despite all these hardships, Paul never ceased to preach the Word of God whenever he had the opportunity.

v.2. Letters to the Synagogues—at Damascus there was a large Jewish colony that was to some extent under the jurisdiction of the Sanhedrin.

v.5. "I am Jesus Whom you are persecuting"—by these words the Glorious Jesus in heaven and His members here on earth are identified as one and the same entity. Meditating on these words, St. Paul was later to elaborate a theology of the Mystical Body of Christ.

v.11. The street called *Straight*—this street is still to be found today in Damascus. No more is known of Ananias and Judas than what is written here.

v.15. Verse 15 is reminiscent of the canticle of the Servant of Jahweh in Isaiah (49:1-6; 53). The mention of the sufferings that the Apostle must undergo leads us to believe that Paul was selected to continue the mission and the passion of Jesus.

Acts 9:31-43 THE PASTORAL JOURNEY OF ST. PETER

The Church (this term is now to be understood as meaning the universal Church) increased in member-

63

ship and consequently St. Peter made a pastoral visit to the new converts, strengthening them in their faith by miracles and healings of the same type that Jesus had worked (note the similarity between the expressions *"Thalita qumi"* and *"Tabita qumi"*). The principal reason for this short account, however, is to place St. Peter in the vicinity of Caesarea where there will take place one of the most important events in the whole of St. Luke's narrative.

Joppa, modern Jaffa, lay northwest of Jerusalem and was the most important part of southern Palestine. Lydda lay between Joppa and Jerusalem; Caesarea is the harbor to the north of Joppa.

v.41. The saints and widows—the faithful were usually called "saints," but the title referred especially to the community in Jerusalem. "Widows," according to 1 Tim. 5:3-16, were elderly women who, after the death of their husbands, dedicated themselves to the works of mercy, caring for their fellow Christians. Here it seems that they attended Tabita in her illness.

* * * * *

CHAPTER 10

Acts 10:1-11:18 THE ADMISSION OF THE GENTILES INTO
THE CHURCH

The human race, according to the Hebrews, was
divided into two distinct categories: the Jews and the
Gentiles. The Gentiles, or non-Jews, were considered
by almost all rabbis to be spiritually lost, unclean and
impure. The Pharisees did not even allow a Jew to
enter the house of a pagan, let alone sit at the same
table and eat with him. The only way that the *"gojim"*
could win social acceptance from the Jews was by
being circumcised and by submitting to the rigors of
the Mosaic Law. They were then classed as proselytes
or converts, but were still considered by the rabbis as
second-class Jews. In between there were those pagans
who were known as "God-fearers" (10:2). They sym-
pathized with the Jews and worshipped the One True
God, but were willing neither to be circumcised nor to
obey the Law. They were admitted to the synagogue

65

to listen to the Bible readings, but they were still considered Gentiles.

The Prophets of old, who witnessed the infidelity of their own people, prophesied that God would call a New People in the future, a people composed of faithful Jews and the neighboring nations, a people that would join together in a pilgrimage to Mt. Sinai to adore Jahweh (Is. 2:3; 19:23; 40:5; 45:20; 55:5; 62:10; Hos. 1:10; 2:23). The rabbis knew these texts, but they thought that this New People of God would be composed of converts to Judaism, a people with circumcision and submissive to the Mosaic Law: this is why they energetically dedicated themselves to proselytizing (Mt. 23:15).

Christ followed in the footsteps of the Prophets by foretelling the conversion of the Gentiles within the framework of the great eschatological pilgrimage (Lk. 13:28; Mt. 8:11). The Risen Christ left no doubt about His universally salvific will, commanding His Apostles to go and preach to all nations baptizing them in the Name of the Father and of the Son and of the Holy Spirit (Mt. 28:18).

The primitive Church was quick to understand the words of Christ as well as those of the Prophets, but there were many who still were influenced by rabbinical tradition and remained convinced that the Gentiles would have to enter the Church only by first being circumcised and submitting to the Law of Moses.

The question was resolved by God Himself when

He called the pagan Cornelius. The account given by Luke is long and detailed, with many repetitions intended to underline the importance of the event. It unfolds like a drama in four acts: first in Caesarea, then in Joppa, Caesarea again, and finally Jerusalem. Directed exclusively by the Holy Spirit, Peter had nothing to do but to obey and follow the signs which the Spirit manifested to him. The vision of the unclean animals made Peter understand that he had nothing to fear from God for socializing with the Gentiles. The Hebrews were prohibited from eating certain types of meat; in this vision the pagans were compared to these unclean animals, but Peter was reminded that God had purified them and that they were no longer unclean (10:15).

The Prince of the Apostles heeded the voice of the Spirit and set out for the house of Cornelius where he preached the message of salvation effected by the death and resurrection of Christ. Cornelius and his family believed and immediately the Holy Spirit descended upon them just as He had descended upon the disciples on Pentecost, revealing that salvation was meant for the Gentiles also. God had forgiven them their sins and had justified them by His Grace. Peter could question no more—he had to obey the Holy Spirit and baptize them.

But that was not all. The faithful of the "circumcision," in other words, those Hebrew Christians who still believed that there was no other way to Christ except through circumcision, harshly rebuked Peter for having entered the house of a pagan and for having baptized him without first having circumcised him. Peter defended himself by relating the vision revealed to him by God, and by referring to the testimony of the six disciples who had been with him in Cornelius' house. The Christian Jews humbly accepted this vision as a sign from God and the question seemed settled once and for all.

But such was not the case. If, on the one hand, Peter had convinced some, there were still many others who were opposed to admitting pagans into the Church, maintaining that they had to become Jews first. At the time when Luke was writing, this error was very widespread, so much so that it warranted such a detailed defense against this group of Judaistic Christians.

v.1. Italian cohort—the troops stationed in the provinces were generally auxiliaries; we know that the Second Italian Cohort was composed of volunteers.

v.2. a devout man—faith is a gift from God which is unmerited. However, St. Luke insists that there is still necessary in any conversion a moral predisposition which is such that the person is psychologically disposed to receive this gift.

v.12. Animals and reptiles, etc.—all the unclean animals that were prohibited by the Law.

v.46. Speaking in tongues and extolling God—it was the very same miracle that manifested the presence of the Holy Spirit on Pentecost, and which repeated itself frequently among the early Christians.

*   *   *   *   *

CHAPTER 11

Acts 11:19-30 THE FIRST GREEK COMMUNITY

What the Prophets had foretold was taking place. The Chosen People were unfaithful to God. They persisted in denying Christ and continued to persecute the Church; they "resisted the Holy Spirit" as Stephen had once said, wherefore salvation was offered to the Gentiles. Thus the New People of God took form, composed of both Jews and Gentiles whose hearts had been opened to the Good-News. The Christians, dispersed by the persecutions described in Acts 8:1, preached Christ in Antioch, where the first mixed community took shape. Since these believers no longer belonged to the synagogue, they were soon called by the new name of "Christians" or those who believed that Jesus was the Christ. Luke insists that the community at Jerusalem, which was still the heart of the Church, took a strong interest in this new type of community, especially after Peter's experience with Cornelius. Barnabas, who was sent to confirm the

71

new believers in their faith, came to Antioch, thus linking them with the center in Jerusalem.

The episode of the famine underlines still more strongly the bond that united the two communities. The Christians of Jerusalem, otherwise known as "the Saints," handed on the fullness of their spiritual heritage to the newly-converted, who in turn helped the poor in Judea with their material contributions. With a deft stroke of the brush, the artist Luke paints us a picture of the unity and the bond that existed between the Jews and the Greeks in the nascent Church. The New People of God foretold by the Prophets in the eschatological era was already in a state of formation.

v.19. Phoenicia—a strip of land along the Mediterranean proceeding from Mt. Carmel and continuing upwards.

v.19. Antioch—this famous city on the Orontes was the "third of the great cities of the Roman Empire," as important as it was beautiful. The foundation of a community in such a city attests to the great leap forward that Christianity had made.

v.21. The Hand of the Lord—The Holy Spirit Who directed the expanding Church.

v.28. Famine—probably the same one Josephus speaks about (*Ant.* XX, 2, 5) which took place in 46-48 A.D.

v.30. Elders—Leaders of the Church in Jerusalem.

* * * * *

CHAPTER 12

Acts 12:1-25 THE KINGS OF HISTORY AND THE HISTORY
OF SALVATION

The passion of the Church continues. The name
of Herod (short for Herod Agrippa I) and the mention
of the Pasch remind us of the Passion of Jesus and
this should not surprise us at all. The present pericope
brings to light the fact that the Word of the Gospel
and the development of the Church are not subject
to the normal patterns of history. God has specific plans
regarding the salvation of men, and even kings are
subject to them. If they do not cooperate, God will
find other ways of obtaining His will; but woe to those
who oppose His designs.

The hour of James, the brother of John and the
son of Zebedee, had come, and the Apostle submitted
himself to the will of God, bearing witness with his
own blood. God, however, had other plans for Peter,

73

and so He freed him in a very simple way despite all
the precautions that Herod and his guards had taken.

Whoever opposes the will of God makes himself
god in some way. And this is exactly what Agrippa
did. As contrasted with what Peter had done when
Cornelius prostrated himself before him (10:25),
Agrippa did not decline the title "God" attributed to
him by the people. Josephus Flavius himself (*Ant.*
XIX 8,2) attributed Herod's ignominious and smarting
death to this very fact, even though he does not mention that Herod went to Caesarea to participate in the
quinquennial games held in honor of the Roman Emperor. It was clear to both Jews and Christians that the
true King of history was Jesus Christ. The rulers of
the world come and go, "but the Word of God will
continue to grow and spread."

v.12. Mary, the mother of John Mark—a wealthy
woman in whose house the Christians held their
liturgical gatherings. John Mark accompanied
Barnabas and Paul on their first missionary journey and it was he who wrote the second Gospel.

v.17. James—cousin of Jesus and bishop of Jerusalem.

v.19. Herod ordered that they should be put to death—
a guard who failed in his duty received the same
sentence as the person whom he was guarding.

v.20. Tyre and Sidon—two thriving Phoenecian cities
north of Caesarea.

* * * * *

CHAPTER 13

Just as Jesus had begun His preaching with the baptism of the Holy Spirit, and the Church began her mission with Pentecost, so the great Apostle to the Gentiles was called explicitly by the Holy Spirit from whom he received a special power, that his preaching would not be "in the plausible words of Wisdom, but in the demonstration of the Spirit and power, that your faith might not rest in the wisdom of men but on the power of God" (1 Cor. 2:4 f).

This power of the Holy Spirit immediately comes to light as we read about Paul's encounter with the magician Bar-Jesus, who, in a certain way, represents the Jewish people. Blinded temporarily, he attempts to leave the Gentiles in the darkness too (Rom. 11:25; 2 Cor. 3:12-18).

75

v.1.   Prophets and teachers—the prophets had a charismatic gift of the Holy Spirit to help them exhort and prophesy in the name of the Lord. The teachers, on the other hand, explained doctrine and morals. The five mentioned here probably form the group of elders of the Antiochian Church.

v.5.   In the synagogues of the Jews—every Sabbath the Jews of every city gathered together in their local synagogues where they prayed, read selections from Scripture, and listened to what some member of the congregation had to say. As there was a custom of granting the word to visiting strangers, Paul made good use of the opportunity to read certain passages from the Old Testament and so be able to preach Christ. He always did this in his travels, unless the Jews became hostile towards him, whereupon he would turn to the Gentiles.

v.6-8.   Proconsul Sergius Paulus—a proconsul governed a senatorial province. Sergius Paulus had been named proconsul of Cyprus in 46 A.D. and had his headquarters at Paphos.

v.7.   Elymas—it is not clear how Elymas justifies the name Bar-Jesus.

v.9.   Saul, who is also called Paul—every Jew of the Diaspora had two names: one Hebrew and the other Greek. Here Luke begins to use the Greek

76

name for Saul, which is Paul, because Paul's
mission is henceforth to the Hellenistic world.

Acts 13:13-52 GOD'S GIFT TO ISRAEL

Paul's discourse in the synagogue of Pisidian Antioch
is a masterpiece of theological apologetic representing
the most acute anti-Jewish polemic of the primitive
Church. The discourse is very similar to that of Peter
in Acts 2, but it is also more elaborate and contains
some final touches which point to arguments treated
by Paul in his Epistles.

In vv.16-22, Paul synthesizes the history of God's
relationship with Israel, beginning with the calling
of Abraham up to the coming of David. This is not
a mere repetition of events already known from the
Bible, but a re-interpretation of the history of the
Jewish people in the light of Christianity. Paul emphasizes the free and merciful initiative of God who
called Abraham and who guided the destiny of His
People, leading them to the summit of their vocation
when He chose David as king, from whom would
descend the Promised Messiah, the Savior of Israel
(v.23).

That Jesus of Nazareth was really the long-awaited
descendant of David is shown by John the Baptist's
witness when he, recognized as the greatest prophet
in all Judea, humbled himself before Christ (vv.24

ff). Unfortunately, the Sanhedrin of Jerusalem, failing to recognize Who He was, condemned Jesus to death, unknowingly fulfilling what the Prophets had said of the Christ and how He had to suffer (Is. 53). They killed Jesus not because He was a criminal. No, He was a Just man, as was His ancestor David—and it was because He was a Just Man that God preserved His body from corruption. God raised Him from the dead and glorified Him, setting Him up as the Messiah to fulfill His promises to the Sons of Israel (vv.26-33).

Paul then continued to strengthen his argument by citing texts from Scripture. He used the texts from Psalm 2:7, Is. 55:3 and Psalm 16:10. Taken together these texts make up the following argument:

> Raising Jesus from the dead and "designating Him Son of God in power" (Rom. 1:3), God fulfilled the prophecy of Isaiah who would have given to Israel the blessing promised to David. Now David had been promised that he would not see the corruption of death, but because he died just as everyone else, the promise still held good for the Messiah who came in the line of David. We, who have already seen the Risen Jesus with our own eyes, preach Him to you, and you have to agree with us that He is the Promised Messiah. What are the practical consequences? The salvation which Christ came to bring us consists in the remission of our sins and our justification before God (vv.

38 f). Till now, the Law of Moses was unable to remove sin, inasmuch as it could only distinguish between what was forbidden and what permitted; it could never do anything to help man in the performance of some good work (Rom. 7:7-25). But if one believes in Christ, his sins will be forgiven him and he will be justified. Here is the essence of the message that God has sent to Israel.

If the Israelites do not accept this message, God will perform the unprecedented act of offering this very same salvation to the Gentiles (vv.40 f; Heb. 1:5).

Actually that is what happened. The Jews listened to the Good News out of mere curiosity, but as soon as they found out that the Gentiles believed, they were infuriated with jealousy and began those tiring persecutions which Paul was to suffer throughout the rest of his life. Israel had rejected Christ's extended hand, and thus salvation was given to the Gentiles.

v.13. Perga in Pamphylia—it seems that Paul did not preach upon his arrival at Perga. It appears that John Mark, afraid of the half-civilized surroundings, departed and returned home.

v.14. Antioch of Pisidia—Antioch was situated in Phrygia in the Roman province of Galatia (the letter to the Galatians was directed to this community also). But because this city was founded by the Romans for the sole purpose of keeping

79

the marauders of Pisidia in check, the city frequently was called Pisidian Antioch.

v.15. The Law and the Prophets—"The Law" was the Pentateuch; "The Prophets" were all the other canonical books. Liturgically speaking these corresponded roughly to our "Gospel" and "Epistle" (cf. Lk. 4:16-21).

v.16. Men of Israel, and you that fear God—Paul spoke to the Jews, and to the Jewish sympathizers who believed in God but were not yet circumcised.

v.20. About four hundred and fifty years—an uncertain text, referring perhaps to a rabbinical tradition.

v.48. As many as were ordained to eternal life—those whom God had chosen as His New People after His Chosen People prevaricated.

* * * * *

CHAPTER 14

Acts 14:1-28 PAUL AMONG THE GENTILES

When Mary presented Jesus in the Temple, Simeon had foretold that the Child would be a sign of contradiction (Lk. 2:34) in Israel. This prophecy was not restricted to Christ's physical Person alone, but included his Mystical Body as well. The Church is a sign of contradiction, because She preaches the Gospel of Jesus. This can be seen very clearly in Acts, where Luke takes special note of it each time. In the present chapter (v.4) Paul's preaching divides his audience into believers and non-believers: a thing that happened frequently, sometimes consoling the Apostles, but more often causing them many sufferings. The Church continually grew, though She was constantly harassed by her enemies.

It is interesting to note that the reaction of the

Gentiles to Paul's miracle was very different from that of the Jews in general. Seeing how the crippled man was healed, the Lycaonians thought Paul and Barnabas were gods. As Peter had already done and Herod refused to do (Acts 10:26; 12:22), Paul hastened to add that he was a man like the rest of them; it was Jesus Who had worked the miracle. This incident gave him a chance to preach to the Lycaonians, and his sermon, in its compactness, is without doubt an excellent example of the classic kerygma delivered to the Gentiles by missionaries of the primitive Church.

Paul's sermon was directed against idolatry. Here it was not a question of preaching Jesus the Messiah, since Paul's audience did not yet know of the true God. So the miracle is used to prove that the gods of the Gentiles were "empty things," utterly futile, lacking any real existence whatsoever. The God Whom the Apostle preached is the True God, who exists and created this world. Jahweh revealed Himself in Israel's history, giving her a positive law. To the pagans of other nations, God never made an extraordinary revelation, but, on the hand, neither can we say that He remained hidden from them, for the daily providence that embraces them and fills their hearts with joy comes from God, who, by revealing Himself a good and merciful God, now directly calls them. This passage concerning the history of salvation reverberates in the discourse of the Areopagus (Acts 17:22-31) and in the Letter to the Romans (1:18 ff).

To spoil Paul's obvious success, the Jews suddenly intervene and stone him. The Apostle himself draws the conclusion (v.22): "Through many tribulations we must enter the Kingdom of God." If the Master suffered, must the disciple not suffer likewise?

v.1. Iconium—an important city of Lycaonia. From Pisidian Antioch, Paul proceeded south-east preaching in the Lycaonian cities of Iconium, Lystra and Derbe; all three were situated in the southern part of the Roman province of Galatia.

v.12. Zeus and Hermes—Hermes, being a heavenly messenger, was the god of eloquence. Barnabas, because of his imposing and silent figure, was mistaken for the god of gods, Zeus or Jupiter.

v.13. Oxen and garlands—animals were ringed with flowers before being sacrificed.

v.19. They stoned Paul—the Apostle himself recalls this episode in 2 Cor. 11:25, where he also mentions all the dangers he encountered in the mountains and deserts of that region.

v.22. Kingdom of God—here it refers to the glory inherited by the just after death.

v.23. They appointed Elders—in every city they evangelized, the Apostles appointed a "college of presbyters," which, with the help of deacons, taught, ruled and conducted liturgical prayer. Later, with the death of the Apostles, one of the presbyters, known in Greek as *"episkopoi"* (over-seers), was eventually entrusted with the office of what we have come to know as "bishop."

* * * * *

CHAPTER 15

Acts 15:1-35 THE CENTRAL PROBLEM OF ACTS

The first converts to Christianity were mainly Jews, many of whom were once Pharisees. Naturally they were all circumcised: they continued to circumcise their offspring, and to observe the Mosaic Law. We have already seen what commotion was caused in the primitive Church each time a Gentile was received into the community. Peter appealed to the direct intervention of the Holy Spirit and thus, temporarily at least, resolved the problem. However, concord could not have possibly reigned very long, if we remember how deeply rooted ancient traditions were in the heart of the common Jew. Many could not even imagine a Gentile entering the Church without first being circumcised and embracing the Law of Moses.

This was not merely a practical question. It went

much deeper. Did the Law of the Old Testament not retain its validity together with the Christian faith? It required Paul's theological insight to answer the objection effectively: if we say that we are justified by our own merits, then the Incarnation and the death of Christ are really of no value; if this were so, we could have very well carried on with the Mosaic Law (Gal. 5:2-12). We have only to read Galatians and Romans to see how exhaustively Paul treats this question. St. Luke was faced with the same problem; only he solved it in a different way, employing a historico-theological approach, arriving, however, at the same conclusions as Paul.

Chapter 15 marks the apex of the Book of Acts. Its content, in fact, coincides with the central theme of the entire Book, and its importance is all the more emphasized by the Council of Jerusalem—which itself marks the final and complete break with Judaism. That which had once been only an external break with the Synagogue, now became an internal and final break with the essence of Judaism. The cases of Cornelius and Stephen led to some theological conclusions of great import, such as the doctrine of justification which, by means of faith apart from the Law, was sanctioned officially by the Apostles.

Luke also intended this chapter as an apologia against the Jews and Judaizers of his time, and therefore weaves into the discourses some scriptural arguments which were current in his own day. The whole consequently assumes an "up-to-date" form in perfect Lucan style. Note for example that the scriptural arguments used by Luke are based on the Septuagint; James, would have quoted the Hebrew text. Still this does not lessen the fact that the discourses preserve their historical core.

The difficulty of reconciling this chapter with what St. Paul says in Gal. 2:1-14 is classical. Luke tells us that the Apostles and presbyters held a meeting in Jerusalem to resolve once for all the question about the conversion of the Gentiles. A compromise was reached whereby the Gentiles were obliged to observe four prescriptions (vv.23-29). St. Paul, on the other hand, never mentions any conditions whatever in his letters; in fact, from the context of Gal. 2; 1 Cor. 8-10, and Rom. 14, he seems to ignore them altogether. Later on (Acts 21:25), James speaks to Paul about these prescriptions, presupposing that the Apostles knew nothing about them. Yet we learn from Acts 15:22 that it was Paul who carried the letter to Antioch and that it was he who announced the decisions of the "Council" in Lycaonia (Acts 16:14). Many solutions have been brought forward to untangle this discrepancy. We hold that the events narrated did take place, but in different time-sequence. First there was the sole discussion of the necessity of circumcision and the Law. Peter and Paul taught and preached that faith and Baptism, not the Mosaic Law, sufficed for salvation (here we are not talking about the different observances of the Mosaic Law). In practice, however, many difficulties arose, as we read in Gal. 2:11-14, where Paul even reprimanded Peter.

The problem was taken up again, probably in Paul's absence, and a new agreement was reached with certain prescriptions whereby the Jewish-Christians were able to overcome their repugnance against joining the Gentiles at table. This decision reached Paul and Barnabas a little later (Acts 21:25) and Paul would have eventually preached it on his later trips. Luke simply squashed these events into a two-dimensional outline, emphasizing the theological arguments rather than the time-sequence. He did the very same thing when he wrote about Christ's journey up to Jerusalem; so did St. Matthew when he knit together the "Sermon on the Mount."

Peter's argument in defense of freedom from the Law was the following (Acts 15:7-11):

> God Himself, Who chose us to preach to the Gentiles and justified them without circumcision (Cornelius' case), has borne witness that He treats Jews and Gentiles alike. Neither is saved through circumcision, but through faith. If we now were to impose the yoke of the Law, we would be affronting God and doubting His very word (cf. Gal. 3:2). Practically speaking the Law is already an insupportable burden, and if the Jews do not even observe it, how can we expect the Gentiles to do so?

88

The Law then was superfluous, not only for the Gentiles, but also for the Jewish-Christians.

James' discourse evinces the same arguments as Peter's. God had spoken through Amos (9:11 ff, [LXX]) promising that He would select His People from among the Gentiles. The admittance of the Gentiles into the Church was taking place according to the divine plan. In practice then, the Christian Jews were to treat the Gentile converts as Gentile proselytes who always resided among them in Israel (Lev. 17-18). Because of their regular attendance at the synagogues, the Gentile converts were already familiar with the four basic prescriptions they had to observe, viz: (1) they had to refrain from food which, after having been offered to idols, was sold in shops; (2) they were to refrain from entering into a marriage of forbidden degrees; (3) the flesh of suffocated animals was prohibited; (4) meat containing blood, the symbol of life—and life belongs to God alone—was also forbidden. Some codices give only three prescriptions: idolatry, fornication and homicide, but these codices, written by a scribe who was not very familiar with Hebrew customs, are not very persuasive and so do not apply here.

With the conclusion of this episode, the Church had resolved once and for all the gravest problem to beset her during her short history and estrangement from Israel. The Church had thus taken a big step forward in understanding herself as a separate community having her roots in Judaism, but her very foundation in Christ alone. No longer would the restrictions of Judaism keep the Church from her goal of conquering the entire world.

* * * * *

CHAPTER 16

Acts 15:36-16:5 THE GENTILE HARVEST AFTER THE
"COUNCIL"

As sometimes happens, divers opinions can arise
even between saints and at times with drastic results,
without, however, destroying the bond of charity. Paul
did not think Mark was bold enough to accompany him
on his coming missionary journey. The Holy Spirit,
in His Providence foreseeing the evangelization of
all Europe, chose a worthy instrument in the person
of Silas who accompanied Paul on his first missionary
journey (Acts 15:22,27).

Luke continues telling us that another disciple,
Timothy, was chosen who would also accompany Paul
on the same important journey. Timothy, the son of
a Hebrew mother and a Gentile father, was not circumcised, and was therefore considered an apostate by
the Jews. Although there was no theological reason to
circumcise him, Paul with a liberty befitting the Sons

of God and with that certain flexibility so helpful to him in his mission to the Gentiles, foresaw the practical consequences and did not hesitate to act.

Acts 16:6-15 THE GOSPEL REACHES EUROPE

The preaching of the Word of God was about to make a great leap forward: from Asia Minor it moved across to Europe. Paul, intending to preach in the provinces of Asia and Bithynia, never thought of the possibility. But the Holy Spirit, like a general at war planning his strategy, banned him from Bithynia and compelled him to go to Troas. There the Spirit of Jesus again manifested to him His will—this time more positively in a dream. Paul had to cross over into Greece, not only the cultural, but also the pagan center of the world. He obeyed, and for the first time in the Acts, the scene is played on a Hellenic stage. Luke gives a detailed account of the conversions made there: there was a Gentile woman "who feared God," and the Spirit, having directed the preaching of the Gospel up to this point, "opened her heart to give heed to what was said by Paul" (v.14). Even in Greece the Jews were the first to be evangelized, but again the Gentiles were the first to believe.

v.10. Sought to go on—here is the first time Luke speaks in the first person plural, sign that he has already joined Timothy, Silas and Paul.

v.12. Philippi—verse 12 is probably a corrupt text and should read: "Philippi, a city of the principal region of Macedonia, a colony." Macedonia was divided into four provinces, each with a quasi-independent governor. Philippi was the first province. Luke mentions also that it was a colony, thereby preparing the readers for what is to come.

v.13. To the riverside—those Jews who had no synagogue used to hold their meetings on the banks of a river to facilitate ritual ablutions.

Acts 16:16-40 THE CIVIL AUTHORITIES

Satan himself had already testified that Jesus was the Son of God (Lk. 4:33; Mk. 1:23). The divining spirit of the pagan girl professed the same thing, having recognized Paul and proclaiming that the wisdom and the power of Christianity were by far superior to the power of the Gentiles: true salvation is now in the hands of the Apostles.

Paul and Silas' imprisonment re-echoes that of Peter's in Jerusalem. The persecution of the Church continues, only now it is not the Jews who are the cause but those who are interested only in themselves and their lucrative business.

Paul and Silas were accused of preaching a religion which was not sanctioned by the state: an accusation definitely out of date which would not have occurred to anyone but those bent on finding some fault. Actually

93

the fact that Claudius had at that time exiled the Jews from Rome favored the accusation, for the prosecutors made it a point to mention that Paul and Silas were Jews. An official condemnation would certainly have been a heavy blow against the progress of evangelization. Hence God Himself bore witness in their favor. As it turned out, the civil authorities found nothing on which to base the accusations, and even the fact that the jailer was converted testified to Paul and Silas' innocence. Here Luke begins a series of apologias, showing how the civil authority, above all, the Roman civil authority, never once found anything wrong with Christianity. On the contrary, the authorities often took the defense of Christianity.

v.37. Roman citizens—Paul was born a Roman citizen (22:28). His father had acquired this privilege by performing some public or economic service for the state. The "Lex Porcia" and the "Lex Julia" forbade the flogging of Roman citizens. The magistrates would have been punished severely had not Paul withdrawn his complaint. For the Apostle it was enough that the Gospel be publicly vindicated.

* * * * *

CHAPTER 17

Acts 17:1-15 THE JEWS AND SCRIPTURE

When St. Luke says that "the Lord opened Lydia's heart to give heed to what Paul was saying" (16:14), he explicitly intended to tell us that faith is a gift from God. St. Paul himself tells us very often that we are "called," not because of any merits on our part, but because of the boundless mercy of God. At the same time, however, this "call" by God is closely connected with other factors which presuppose a certain psychological disposition, before this precious gift is received. Luke frequently insists on the necessity of such a disposition, as we shall see later on, and with his usually apologetic manner he describes how Paul worked many miracles; always however, among the pagans. The Jews had the Scriptures to bear witness, but "If they do not hear Moses and the Prophets, neither will they be convinced if one should rise from the dead" (Lk. 16:31). At Thessalonica Paul proved from the Prophets that Christ was the Messiah. The Jews there refused to believe. At Berea Paul found the Jews "more noble than those of Thessalonica, for they received the word with all eagerness, examining the Scriptures daily to see if these things were so" (Acts 17:11).

Like the unbelieving Jews of Jerusalem who had delivered Jesus to the civil authorities, accusing Him of trying to make Himself king, the Jews of Thessalonica brought Paul before the magistrates, charging him with preaching another king. Moreover, Paul and Silas were charged with "turning the world upside down" (the very accusation Claudius had made against the Jews themselves) and acting against the decrees of Caesar. Claudius had ordered that the synagogue cult in the Empire was not to be disturbed. As occurs often in the Acts, these fallacious arguments came to naught and the civil authorities freed the Apostles.

v.1. Thessalonica—Capital of Macedonia, residence of five or six "magistrates," which is the technical term in v.6.

v.6. Jason—a convert from Judaism, who offered Paul hospitality, possibly the relative of Paul mentioned in Rom. 16:21.

* * * * *

This is another prominent aspect of the Book of Acts. The Word of the Gospel has been brought to Athens, the cultural center of the Hellenistic world. In verses 16-21 Luke sets the stage for the oncoming encounter between the "folly of the Cross" and the "wisdom of the world" (1 Cor. 1:20). We know in advance that Paul's preaching will not have immediate success; the Stoics lacked the necessary humility and the Epicureans were too materialistic to be able to listen profitably to the word of Him Who was obedient even to His death on the Cross. Both schools like to listen to debates not out of any genuine thirst for the truth, but out of mere curiosity and a craving for novelty. Christianity, they soon discovered, was not a philosophy composed of brilliant theories, but the humble Word of God which required faith and obedience.

Paul's discourse, a typical example of the "kerygma" preached to the Gentiles (as in Acts 14) contains biblical ideas expressed in terms of the then current Greek philosophy. Luke the apologist takes advantage of this tradition to instruct his readers in the method of presenting the Gospel to the Gentiles. The following briefly outlines the discourse:

You think your consciences are now at ease because you have erected altars to everyone of your gods.

97

Your religious enthusiasm is indeed praiseworthy, but unfortunately you have a mistaken notion of the Divine Nature. The God that I preach to you is far different from any of your mythical gods (v.23). He is the One True God Who created the entire universe and it is He who gave life and breath to all men. God does not dwell in temples built by hands, as if He were in need of our adoration; neither is He served "by human hands," as if we were doing Him a favor by adoring Him. Being the Giver of life, He gave us life even before we had begun to adore Him. The highest worship we could possibly render Him is by thanking Him (Rom. 1:18 ff; Acts 17:25). The True God is not a local or national God, since He is the Father of the entire human race, which finds its origin in Adam, His son, whom He had created and from whom all of us are descended. God also made the various nations of the earth, determining their boundaries, providing and sustaining them with rains and fruitful seasons (Acts 14:16). Each one of us, then, because of all these signs and blessings around us, has the duty "to search for" this God, to reflect and meditate on His nature and goodness, to seek to do His will (v.27). This is not easy, but neither is it impossible; groping for Him, we will find Him, since He is not far away from any one of us: in fact, the universe is filled with His presence and power (v.28). Moreover, God is our

Father and we are His offspring (v.28). He has made us, not we Him as the pagans seem to imply. Consequently you have to admit that you have erred gravely; you never found the True God, because, believing all along that He was made of stone or silver, and that He lived in the temples you erected, you thought you were doing Him a favor by adoring Him. Believing that there are many gods and that the Divinity is especially far from you, you are gravely mistaken. The God that I am preaching to you is willing to overlook your error; your ignorance will be utterly forgotten if you but return, come back to a proper idea of the Divinity, and conform your lives to God's will (v.30). He has already chosen a Man, who, risen from the dead, will come to judge you (v.31). The Risen Christ is the Savior, but He is also the Supreme Judge.

CHAPTER 18

v.18. The Resurrection—they believed *"Anastasis"* was a new Goddess.

v.19. The Areopagus—the hill of Mars, northwest of the Acropolis, seat of the "Council" of the Areopagus which judged homicide cases and which later on controlled pedagogy in the State.

v.23. To an Unknown God—even to this day archaeologists have not found a similar inscription, or if they have, it has been in the plural form "To the Unknown Gods."

v.25. He gave to all men life and breath and everything—an obvious quotation from Isaiah 42:5, with, however a slight change: "spirit" is changed into "breath" and "people" into "all men," probably to avoid any misinterpretation. The "Spirit" was given only to the "Chosen People."

v.28. Some of your poets—Aratus of Soli (in Cilicia) in an ode to Jupiter.

101

v.34. Dionysius the Areopagite—traditionally believed to be the first bishop of Athens. Under his name many neo-platonic writers of the early patristic period disseminated their ideas which ultimately came to bear a tremendous influence on mediaeval theology.

* * * * *

Acts 18:1-22 FROM THE JEWS TO THE GENTILES

The central theme of Acts, that salvation was given to the Gentiles because the Jews rejected it, gains momentum and strength. The present account, with its numerous details, shows that Paul, practicing certain plainly Jewish prescriptions, still considers himself as a Jew. In fact, it is the Israelites and not the Christians, who, blaspheming Christ, have fallen from outside the true Israel. These children of contradiction will incur the curse: "His blood be on us and on our children" (v.6; cf. Mt. 27:25). Paul thus left the Jews and went to the Gentiles, even living with them, to emphasize the transition still more (v.7). Among them he had great success. The Lord Himself had promised him that there would be in Corinth a multitude of people who would believe, chosen not according to race or merits, but according to grace.

The verdict of Gallio is the usual argument given

by Luke to show that the civil authority not only did not interfere with the doctrines of Christianity, but positively acted in favor of the Church, not finding anything wrong with its practices.

v.2. Aquila and Priscilla—cf. Acts 18:26; Rom. 16:3-5; 2 Tim. 4:19.

v.2. Claudius—in the year 49/50, Claudius expelled the Jews from Rome because of certain dissensions in their communities.

v.3. Tent-makers—a common occupation in Tarsus, a large commercial center for tents made of hides. Paul labored with his own hands so that he would not burden his community (cf. Acts 20:34).

v.12. Gallio—the elder brother of the philosopher, Seneca, and proconsul of Achaia in 51/52.

v.13. Law—can be understood as the Jewish Law, in which case the accusation would refer to the concession made by Claudius; namely, that the Jews were to be able to worship freely; or it can refer to Roman Law, which prohibited anyone from practicing a foreign religion not formally approved by the State.

v.17. Sosthenes—this anti-semitic demonstration did not interest Gallio; the scales were turned and the accusers were the ones who lost face.

v.18. He cut his hair—it was the custom for Jews to make a vow (the so-called Nazarite vow) to obtain some favor from God. They were to abstain

from wine, let their hair grow and not have it
cut before they sacrificed in the temple.

v.22. The Church—The Jerusalem community, still
considered the "Church" par excellence.

CHAPTER 19

Acts 18:23-19:7 THE DISCIPLES OF JOHN

The movement originated by John the Baptist seems to have gained supporters among the Jews of the Diaspora as well. Pilgrims to Jerusalem had heard him preaching penance and preparation for the Kingdom of God. On their return to their homeland, they too preached the same message, remaining faithful to their vows and awaiting the Kingdom of the Messiah. Many of them had never heard of Jesus in particular, and others, as we gather from the episode related in Lk. 7:19 ff, still maintained doubts about Christ's Messiahship, since they interpreted wrongly the signs of the coming of the Messiah. Such disciples were still numerous during the lifetime of the Apostles, and probably also at the time of Luke himself who uses the story about Apollo and the twelve converts apologetically against some Johannine groups of his own time.

This account of Apollo ties up closely with what we already know of him from 1 Cor. 3, but it is possible that Paul's encounter with the twelve disciples of John occurred at another time, and that Luke relates it here to emphasize his theological arguments. Apollo, a man well-versed in the Scriptures, and from Alexandria, where the great Philo had founded a school of allegorical interpretation, had one thing in common with the other twelve—he "believed," but his knowledge, like theirs, was still imperfect. They were sincere men, having already received John's baptism, which was not a sacrament, as it only signified the Messianic reality but did not confer that Messianic salvation. It disposed the soul to receive the great gift of the age of fulfillment, the Holy Spirit.

The disciples already well disposed to a Messianic understanding of the Scriptures, morally in order, and already awaiting the coming of the Anointed One, had only to receive the last necessary instruction to be converted. They found themselves on the threshold of Christianity, behind them was the promise, ahead was the fulfillment. Their rejoinder to Paul, "We have never even heard that there is a Holy Spirit" (Acts 19:2), reveals the drought caused by the absence of that great sign and gift of salvation which comes only through the Baptism of Jesus.

The argument used to convince them did not consist merely in the testimony of John himself, but especially in the answer Jesus gave to John's disciples in Lk. 7:19 ff. Naturally, what really convinced them was the vehemence of the Holy Spirit which they experienced in their souls: as soon as they were baptized they "spoke with tongues and prophesied" (Acts 19:6). This experience was constantly referred to by the Apostles as the basic argument for the presence of the eschatological era (Gal. 3:2 f).

* * * * *

Acts 19:8-22 EPHESUS—THE APEX OF MISSIONARY SUCCESS

Paul's mission to the Gentiles reached its zenith at Ephesus. Having withdrawn with his disciples from the unbelieving Jews of that city, he began to extend his mission to the province of Asia in and around Ephesus, and this he did with considerable success. Before, as we recall, the Holy Spirit had forbidden Paul to preach in Asia (Acts 16:6). Now the time of their calling is ripe and the Apostle is sent to bring them salvation.

Miracles were many. Pieces of cloth that had touched Paul healed the sick, as the garments of Christ (Lk. 6:19) and the shadow of Peter had done (Acts 5:15). Meanwhile, Judaism was rendered powerless. Even the sons of the High Priest could no longer prevail over the evil spirits. What was needed to overcome the powers of Satan was the Name of Jesus pronounced

107

by the Church. Pagan magicians do not find themselves in better circumstances. Many, both Jews and Gentiles, acknowledging their utter helplessness before the Almighty Power of the Holy Spirit, burned a heap of magical books, valued at over fifty thousand pieces of silver ($8000).

Once Paul had reached the peak of missionary success, however, his life-star began to wane. He sets his face towards Jerusalem, as Jesus had done after the culmination of His success in Galilee where He had just driven out a devil, causing great amazement among the crowds. There began His "theological journey" towards the Holy City, where He had to suffer (Lk. 9:51) because "it cannot be that a prophet, should perish away from Jerusalem" (Lk. 13:13)! Paul too will be betrayed in Jerusalem where he will be handed over to the Gentiles to be judged. The parallel between his life and his Master's will now be complete. Thereafter Paul intended to go to Rome (v.21) where the definitive and final transfer of the Gospel from Judaism to the pagan world will be consummated.

* * * * *

Acts 19:23-20:1 THE DECLINE OF THE GODS

With the Jewish exorcists and pagan magicians clearly reduced to helplessness the pagan gods, too, begin to decline. The first sure sign of this is the protest Demetrius made because the little shrines he manufactured and which the people were accustomed to present as votive offerings to the goddess Diana, were no longer selling, thanks to Paul's preaching.

The merchant's protest was useless. He not only could not stop the landslide created by the Gospel, but he unwittingly brought to the defense of Christianity the influential Asiarchs who, as it turned out, saved Paul's life. The people vented their anger against the Jews who undoubtedly were behind the riot, and Alexander was the one to suffer the consequences.

A very winning plea came from the town clerk, who held much influence in Ephesus. According to him, the Christians were neither sacriligious nor blasphemous, and even if they were, this was not the proper way to accuse them; that is what law-courts were for. But even at court Sergius Paulus, the officials of Philippi, Gallio, Festus, Agrippa and all the Roman civil authorities could never find any valid arguments condemning Christianity. Paganism in reality was waging a losing battle. Luke mustered together all these facts and envisioned exactly what would be verified, two centuries later. When Paul himself relates his own sentiments in those circumstances, however, he is not at all exuberant (2 Cor. 1:8 ff). Intent upon visiting Jerusalem, he had realized that his own passion was fast approaching.

v.24. Demetrius—there is an inscription (from the first century) of a certain Demetrius, a financial administrator of the temple at Ephesus. Whether both are identical remains unknown. Statuettes of terra cotta have been found in abundance in the excavations at Ephesus, but there has yet to be found one made of silver—probably because these were melted down by the priests from time to time.

v.24. Artemis—or Diana, the Oriental goddess of fertility, represented with the lower half of her body wrapped somewhat like a mummy, and the upper half covered with a multitude of breasts. Inscriptions usually bear the title "Artemis the Great."

v.31. Asiarchs—historically speaking, the plural form is more exact. Their function however, still remains a puzzle. They probably convened every year in a representative capacity as presidents or ex-presidents.

v.35. The town clerk—was the most influential person in the city, since he was in charge of public assemblies.

v.35. And the sacred stone that fell from the sky—the statue of Diana in the temple was a crude one and was popularly believed to have fallen from heaven (a meteorite, perhaps?).

v.39. Regular assembly—many Greek cities continued the City-State tradition of classical times, when the entire populace met to discuss political and administrative affairs. The Romans later on incorporated the "Council of the People," but since the rulers were suspicious of such assemblies, the town clerks were very conscious to avoid inciting riots.

* * * * *

CHAPTER 20

Acts 20:2-16 THE JOURNEY TO JERUSALEM

Luke continues to draw a parallel between the journey and Jesus' journey to Jerusalem in his Gospel (Lk. 9:51 ff). The group stopped at Troas, where Paul worked a miracle similar to those of Elijah's (1 Kings 17:17-24), Jesus' (Lk. 7:14) and Peter's (Acts 9:36-41). Notice the triptych of Jesus, Peter, and Paul painted by the artist Luke.

The Resurrection of the dead boy symbolized the spiritual resurrection that would accompany the salvation effected by the Messiah. Its meaning is brought out still more when we reflect that the miracle took place during the celebration of the Eucharist, the "Breaking of the Bread."

*   *   *   *   *

Paul's discourse to the Elders of the Church of
Ephesus congregated at Miletus is not only one of the
most moving in the second part of the Acts, but also
one of the most enigmatical. It is completely different
from the kerygmatic-literary genre we have encountered
so far. It rather approximates the literary genre of Paul's
Pastoral Epistles, to which it is akin because of the
noticeable similarity of ideas, feelings, vocabulary and
circumstances. If this discourse was really delivered by
Paul on his third missionary journey (when the Second
Letter to the Corinthians was also written which is
decidedly different in both spirit and style), how do
we explain the fact that Paul told the Ephesians that
they would see his face no more (v.25), when in
1 Tim. 1:3, we are led to believe that the Apostle
visited Ephesus again after his Roman imprisonment?
We can surmise, in any event, that Luke had access to
Paul's farewell address at Miletus only after the martyrdom of the Apostle. Moreover, since Luke had no
intention of recounting Paul's life beyond the Apostle's
arrival at Rome, he inserted this discourse into the
chapter in order to throw his theological argument into
relief, namely, to make the sufferings of the Church
culminate in Jerusalem. Chronologically, the discourse
was probably delivered during Paul's last visit to
Ephesus, between his first and second imprisonment in

114

Rome, more or less the same period during which he either orally or in writing drafted the Pastoral Epistles.

The spiritual-theological value of Paul's discourse lies in the exhortation to the faithful to build their faith on the doctrine and practices inherited from the Apostles. The Twelve, one by one, disappeared from the scene, but they did leave a deposit of faith to be safeguarded and a way of life to be followed by the faithful. Divisions and rash doctrines would soon find their way into the Church, even false prophets would appear, making a lucrative business from their fraudulent teachings. Paul set himself up as an example to be followed: He has preached the true doctrine, working with his own hands to provide for the poor and avoid scandalizing the weak (v.35). He was always looking out for his flock, suffering trials and tribulations, setting an example for those who should carry on his work. The discourse is divided into four parts:

vv.18-21. Despite his sufferings, Paul never once ceased to preach to Greeks and Jews the possibility of salvation through faith and penance.

vv.22-24. The Holy Spirit revealed to Paul that there was more suffering to come. But this did not deter him; he preached the news about the grace of God to the Gentiles, even if it meant that he had to bear the anger and persecution of the Jews.

vv.25-31. If, after all he had preached, someone were

still to flounder and perish, it would not be his fault. There would be fierce wolves both within and without the Church, a reality requiring pastors to be vigilant and firm in the doctrine handed on by the Apostles. These men, Paul continued, were appointed by the Holy Spirit as overseers of the Church, of the very people whom Jesus bought with the price of His own Blood.

vv.32-36. Paul's final blessing: he commends all the faithful to the Almighty Word of God which effects our sanctification and leads us to eternal life. Paul bequeaths to them the maxim: work selflessly because God has saved you selflessly; it is more blessed to give than to receive.

The degree to which Paul was beloved because of his selfless Apostolate was well manifested by the tender farewell given him by the Elders and the faithful.

* * * * *

CHAPTER 21

Acts 21:1-16 THE APPROACHING PASSION

At Miletus, Paul had mentioned that in every city through which he passed, the Holy Spirit had warned him of his forthcoming trial and sufferings in Jerusalem. We know from the Letter to the Romans (15:25-28) that the real reason for this trip was to bring to the brethren in the Holy City the offerings made by the converted Gentiles. Such a collection symbolized the bond of unity between Christian Jews and the Christian Gentiles. Paul did not know that the converted Jews in Jerusalem would refuse the offerings, thereby destroying the bond of unity and love that had hitherto characterized the Church.

Luke, however, is not so much interested in the collection, as he is in describing the coming passion of Paul in Jerusalem, and comparing it with Jesus.' The Holy City is the place where "the prophets who

117

have been sent to her have been stoned and killed" (Lk. 13:34). Already guilty of the death of Christ, Jerusalem was about to consummate her crime by putting the Apostles to death also, consequently meriting her final destruction in the year 70.

Luke knew perfectly well that Paul did not die at Jersualem. But as in the case of Jesus, the apex of Jewish faithlessness is reached when Paul "is delivered into the hands of the Gentiles" (v.11). Jesus also suffered because He was handed over to Pilate (Acts 3:13). For Luke it was sufficient to describe the act of denial. The execution of the sentence is but secondary.

We have already seen how Luke very often emphasizes certain details reminiscent of Christ's own passion, continually reminding us that Christ's passion is prolonged in time through His members. Here we should like to point out some more such parallels: as Jesus had foretold His passion (Lk. 22; 43:45; 18:31, 34), so also did Paul in v.11; v.13 "Why are you weeping so...?" recalls Christ's query to the women of Jerusalem along the way to Calvary (Lk. 23:28 ff); Paul's submission in v.14 mirrors Christ's "Fiat" in Gethsemani (Lk. 22:42).

v.4.   Through the Spirit—the Spirit had prophesied only the passion of Paul; the admonition to bypass Jerusalem, e.g. in v.12, was prompted by Paul's prudent friends.

118

v.10. Agabus—a Christian prophet who performed this symbolic gesture reminiscent of the Prophets of Old (for a classical example, vd. chapter 19 of Jeremiah).

* * * * *

Acts 21:17-26 THE BOND IS STRENGTHENED

The situation in Jerusalem upon Paul's arrival was very touchy. As we saw in the preceding part of this chapter, the Apostle was bringing to the community of Jerusalem the generous contributions made by the Gentile churches. We saw also how much prejudice there was against Paul among some Jewish Christians in Jerusalem because he had preached and written against the Law, circumcision and the meritorious works of the Pharisees. Wherefore Paul had every reason to be apprehensive. Luke himself is caught up in the situation and does his best to recapture the meeting between James and Paul, portraying it as the external sign of the internal unity binding the two Christian communities.

James and the presbyters, understanding Paul's mission and realizing that he was appointed by the Holy Spirit, received him with great joy. But at the same time they feared that the Apostle's mission would be misinterpreted by some who were not well informed. or who were still slaves of the Old Law. That is why

119

James deemed it necessary to posit a compromise. James and Paul agreed on the basic principles: the only thing the Gentiles were to observe was the four prescriptions (commented on in chapter 15), without being bound by any other ceremonial precept of the Law. Paul had also to be on his guard and not scandalize any of the weaker brethren, a principle he himself acknowledged in 1 Cor. 8:13. He must show the Jews that he still respected Jewish traditions. If we recall Acts 18:18, we will see that the Apostle truly had a deep respect for Hebrew traditions, for he was faithful to the vow he had once made to shave his head. There were at that time four local Christians who had made the same vow, but were unable to pay the expenses involved in the ceremony. James beseeched Paul to act as "Godfather." The Apostle concurred, paid the expenses and thereby not only preserved intact, but strengthened, the bond of love existing between the Jewish Christians and converted Gentiles.

* * * * *

Acts 21:27; 22:29 THE GENUINE JEW

Certain Asian Jews, perhaps from Ephesus, who knew Paul, were in Jerusalem and, seeing Paul in the temple, immediately began to denounce him, accusing him of preaching against the Law, the Temple etc., (reminiscent of Stephen's trial). Moreover, they falsely

120

presupposed that Paul had brought a certain uncircumcised Ephesian Gentile within the confines of the Temple. Anyone familiar with the Letters to the Romans, Galatians, and Hebrews, knows very well what truth there was in such accusations. But the second one was unfounded. Paul's accusers vanished from the scene, at least they never appeared to support their accusations in court, thus invalidating them, according to Roman Law.

The Apostle was maltreated by the crowd, and it was the Romans who came to his rescue. Luke, again bringing to the fore his apology, shows how the civil authorities not only did not find anything subversive in Christianity, but they even went so far as to protect it from the accusations of its detractors, the Jews. Moreover, not only did Christianity prove to be innocent of the crimes of those brigands who ever so often created a tumult in Jerusalem (Acts 21:38 f), but they even came from respectable towns and were law-abiding and conscientious citizens. Even Paul's insistence about his Roman citizenship, besides merely explaining why he was not scourged, has an apologetic value intended by Luke, namely, that the Roman authorities acknowledged that among the Christians there were to be found some very worthy citizens, who, even though they believed in Christ, maintained a devotion to their country. We know from history that in the second century, Christianity came to be considered an enemy of the State. Perhaps such ideas were already present

121

at the time Luke wrote the Acts, and he wanted to counteract them.

But the most interesting feature of this part, from a theological point of view, is Paul's discourse to the Jews. The Apostle insisted that he was one-hundred percent Jewish, like many other Christian Jews. Just as faith in Christ was a direct and gratuitous act of God, so now salvation was gratuitously offered to the Gentiles because of the incredulity of the Chosen People. The Christians therefore are the true inheritors of the promises made to the People of God; it is they who continue the true traditions, while the Jews, who were first called, remain steadfast in their disobedience. To emphasize what he had to say, Paul spoke in Hebrew (i.e. in Aramaic, the language of Palestine at the time of Christ). He insisted that he once studied at the feet of Gamaliel (v.13), and that he himself once persecuted the Christians, but by a divine intervention on the road to Damascus he had come to realize his grievous mistake. The vision he had had was not a mere illusion, for it had happened at midday (v.6) and Christ had shone even more radiantly than the sun, so much so that Paul had been blinded (v.11). His witness to the Resurrection, therefore, was truly plausible. Afterwards Jesus had appeared to him in the temple where Jahweh dwelt, warning Paul (because the Jews would not heed his testimony) to leave the city immediately, withdraw to the Gentiles and preach salvation to them. Everything the Apostle did thereafter was prompted by his perfect obedience to the voice of God.

As soon as Paul began to speak on such a delicate matter, the Jews rebelled. To say that the Crucified One was the Messiah was an out-and-out scandal, but to assert and say that God had abandoned His People and called the Gentiles in their stead was just too much! National pride and a deep-rooted antipathy towards the Gentiles blinded and enraged Paul's hearers to the extent that they did not let him finish speaking. Luke had touched on the heart of the theology of the Acts in a very simple way and has left it to his readers to judge.

v.21,27. The seven days—probably refers to a period of time during which a Palestinian Jew who had been outside his homeland and in contact with Gentiles had to spend purifying himself upon his return.

v.21,28. He also brought Greeks into the Temple— within the atrium there was an assigned place for the Gentiles, beyond which they were forbidden to trespass under the penalty of death. The Law protected the Holy Place from contamination.

v.21,30. Out of the Temple—so that they would not contaminate the temple with Paul's blood. The closing of the doors probably symbolizes the Jews' rejection of the apostolic message.

v.21,38. The Egyptian—Josephus Flavius tells us that while Felix was governor, an Egyptian renegade with his band of 600 men stirred up an insurrection in which the majority died, including the renegade head.

CHAPTER 22

v.22,5. Gamaliel—cf. Acts 5:34, note.

v.22,9. Saw the Light—cf Acts 9:7, with which there seems to be a contradiction. Perhaps Paul's companions saw the brilliance without seeing Christ, heard His resounding voice, but did not understand what He said. This is similar to what happened on Mt. Sinai.

v.22,24. Examined by scourging—under torture; but Paul appealed to his rights as a Roman citizen and to his immunity from scourging, just as he had formerly done at Philippi.

v.22,28. A large sum—Roman citizenship could also be obtained by paying a certain sum. As it turned out, Paul was more Roman than his judge!

Acts 22:30-23:11 EXIT JERUSALEM: ENTER ROME

The trial of Paul is the trial of Christianity, and his reply echoes the tenor of the traditional defense of the

Church against the time-worn accusations of the Jews and the ever-present difficulties encountered in the Roman Empire. But Christian apologetics of the first century was meant to convince and invite, not merely to defend. Now the only doctrine that sustained Judaism after the year 70 was that of the Pharisees, and Luke is anxious to show that Christianity, although incompatible with the doctrine of the Sadducees, could be reconciled with Pharisaic teachings, admitting, as they did, the possibility of a resurrection; was not Christianity in fact founded in doctrine and in practice upon the positive truth that a dead Christ really rose and that, because of His Resurrection, we too will rise from the dead?

Paul and Luke did not hesitate to blame the Sanhedrin, the true representatives of Judaism, for the conduct of the Jews towards the Christians. Before the Sanhedrin, Paul had declared that he was acting with a perfectly clear conscience, with the result that, by order of the High Priest, he was struck on the mouth, as Jesus had been (Jo. 18:22). Paul's rebuttal is less meek than was his Master's, but it contains in itself all that the Christians thought of institutional Judaism. Respecting all the while every authority derived from God, they foresaw that the priests who tried to revive a dead and ineffective ritual were doomed because of their resistance "against the Holy Spirit," in Stephen's words. Ananias' malediction was very accurate (he was assassinated by Idumean brigands in 66 A.D.).

126

Jesus had already prophesied that His disciples would be dragged before synagogues, kings, and rulers (Lk. 21:12). The Sanhedrin represented Judaism, while the rulers (Felix), and kings (Agrippa) represented the civil authority, very often pagan, before whom the Church had to explain itself in order to survive. The Apostle bears witness to Jesus in everybody's presence, but Luke is more concerned to show that it is exactly because Paul's witness is not accepted by the Jews in Jerusalem that the Gospel would be preached in Rome, where the Gentiles would accept it. The "Holy City" would be destroyed and would cede its precedence to the "Eternal City." The voice of God, heard from the mouths of the Prophets, the Messiah and the Apostles, had gone unheeded and therefore would resound no longer in that city.

CHAPTER 23

v.2. Ananias—High Priest from the year 47-59, known
for his cruelty and dissolute life. He was murdered
by Idumeans in 66 A.D.
v.5. Cf. Ex. 22:27.

Acts 23:12-35 THE STATE AND THE GOSPEL

The Providence of God uses every possible means
to attain its objective; namely, the world-wide diffusion
of the Gospel. Everything in one way or another was
a factor in bringing the Word of God to Rome. Human
events, which seemed to occur by chance, were really
mapped out on a divine plan. God had guided Israel's
history towards the culminating point of the history of
salvation; now God was directing the activity of His
Church.

Meanwhile Claudius Lysias had affirmed in his
official letter that Paul had perpetrated no crime, and

129

was therefore not guilty of death. The Mosaic Law meant nothing to the Romans, who, Luke says, made it their policy never to interfere in matters purely religious. If any more riots were to occur, the Jews, and not the Christians, would be blamed and punished.

v.16. Son of Paul's sister—Paul had a married sister who lived in Jerusalem, with whom he probably stayed while studying in the Holy City.

v.22. Felix—governor, first of Samaria, then in 52 A.D., of almost all Palestine. He was an ex-slave who suppressed with a brutal hand any "Messianic" movements in Judea. He seduced and married Drusilla, sister of Agrippa II and wife of Azizius, King of Emesa. Paul was brought before Felix in the year 57 A.D.

v.26. Claudius Lysias—a tribune about whom nothing more is known than what is written in the chapter.

v.35. Herod's Praetorium—an echo of the Passion of Jesus.

*   *   *   *   *

CHAPTER 24

An appreciation of the theology of this particular chapter presupposes a knowledge of the personality of the governor Felix. As we already saw, he was a freedman known mainly for the cruelty with which he suppressed the nationalistic insurrections caused by the self-styled "Messiahs." After his brother Pallas, Claudius' treasurer, had fallen from power, Felix, hated by the Jews and no longer aided by his once powerful brother, was replaced by Porcius Festus in the year 60 A.D.

The attorney, Tertullus, knew only too well the psychology of a man like Felix, for with ironic subtleness he tells Felix that "through you we enjoy much peace." Still more, the accusations touched Felix's weakness; Paul was a very active member of a Messianic group, similar to those suppressed by the governor himself. If then the Jews wanted to kill Paul, it was

131

because he had permitted a Gentile to enter the Temple, and even Roman Law permitted the Jews to put to death a Gentile who had transgressed the limits permitted him within the temple. Thus Paul was labelled a ringleader of the "Nazarean Sect." Tertullus, however, was very careful to hide the real reason for the uprising against the Apostle. The Sanhedrin had accused Paul of preaching against the Law, but the fanatical anti-Roman rabble rousers suspected the criticizer of circumcision and of siding with the Romans and Gentiles to whom he preached. In that time of extreme nationalism, this was the real reason for so many murders.

Paul's defense was no less crafty than Tertullus.' No one there could testify that he had ever seen the Apostle at the head of a band of rebels. He was a Jew like the rest of them and he preached a purely spiritual doctrine which had left him with a clear conscience. Actually, Paul continued, there should have been some Jews here from Asia if they really wanted to press the charge against him. But these Jews had vanished from the scene and they could not legally sustain their accusations *in absentia*. Again Paul touched on the delicate question of the resurrection of the dead, which before had caused such discord within the Sanhedrin in Jerusalem. Felix knew Paul's case very well, and realizing that he was on slippery ground, he dismissed the crowd, imprisoned Paul, but kept him in loose custody and did not condemn him. Luke, defending

Paul, notes that the Apostle remained in prison for a long time due to the craving Felix had for popularity, something he could never win from the people. His preoccupation with the defense of the Apostle perhaps best explains why he did not relate the account of Paul's martyrdom during the Apostle's second imprisonment in Rome.

Paul's words were more than instructive for Felix and Drusilla who heard what he preached to them. They were both interested, but when it came to embracing Christianity, they needed more than just an intellectual curiosity; they needed a moral disposition necessary to answer God's call and cooperate with the power of His Word, since the new religion was no mere philosophical theory, but a total surrender to the Lord Jesus. Felix and Drusilla, neither one a model of justice or chastity, were deaf to the call of the Lord and remained in their darkness.

No Roman reading these beautiful pages of Acts would have been able to maintain any prejudices he may have had against Christianity. He might have gone even further and examined his conscience to see if he too did not want to believe and was impeded by the same fears that haunted Felix and Drusilla. Luke was not content with only defending the faith; he also wanted to take the offensive.

v.6. vv.6b,7,8a. are omitted by the majority of reliable manuscripts.

v.14.   Sect—the Christians never admitted that they were a simple sect of Judaism. Their "sect" was "The Way"; it was the others who went astray.

CHAPTER 25

Succeeding Felix in 60 A.D., the new governor, Porcius Felix, (who did not exactly favor the Sanhedrin) a friend of Agrippa, continued to hold Paul prisoner merely to pacify the Jews. But in reality it was he who saved the Apostle from their treachery, refusing to take Paul to Jerusalem for trial. A new motive is now introduced by the Jews as a frantic last-minute accusation—that of the *"Crimen Laesae Majestatis,"* similar to the accusation made against Jesus. Since the provincial governor lacked special power over a Roman citizen accused of *"Crimen Laesae Majestatis,"* Paul was able to appeal to Caesar. The Apostle to the Gentiles made the appeal to avoid falling prey to the cunning of the Jews in Jerusalem; it was really the Providence of God, however, which was maneuvering the actions of men to a realization of the Divine Salvific

135

Plan. The Lord had promised Paul that he would bear witness to Him in Rome; according to the Divine Plan, the occasion now presented itself. Paul is delivered into the hands of the Gentiles. The Jews, reach the height of their unbelief and God ceases to invite them to conversion and offers His gift to the Gentiles, who would respond to His invitation.

* * * * *

Acts 25:13-27 A WITNESS BEFORE KINGS

Even Festus found Paul innocent and clearly stated it to King Agrippa. The Jews who wanted to depict Paul as an enemy of the State were unable to prove their charges; and if the charges could not be proven, the Roman government had no reason to hold the Christians in suspicion or as *personae non gratae*. The charge against Paul was clearly a question pertaining solely to Judaism. This insistence on the innocence of the Apostle in these last six consecutive chapters leaves no doubt about the apologia intended by Luke. The discourses treating of Paul's defense could possibly be Lucan compositions which develop a theme handed on by tradition, a not uncommon technique among the ancients; but the facts are there, and they speak for themselves. Luke reveals himself as a master of apologetics, be it against the Jews or against the Gentiles. At any rate, the Gospel even reached the court of kings, all the while drawing nearer and nearer to Rome.

v.13. Agrippa and Bernice—Agrippa, son of Agrippa I, was seventeen years old when his father died. However, he did not immediately succeed to the throne; in 50 A.D., Claudius gave him a little kingdom in Lebanon. In 53 A.D., he was ruler of the territories of Philip the Tetrarch, of Lysanias and of Caro. Bernice, his sister, was the widow of King Herod of Chalci and at that time was separated from Pelemon, King of Cilicia. She lived, as the concubine of her brother, who, among other things, was an expert in Jewish Law, and very conciliatory in his policies, having strongly opposed the anti-Roman riots.

v.26. Nothing definite to write—naturally when brought before Caesar, Paul had to be accompanied with a letter bearing the charges brought against him. Festus admitted he did not have sufficient material with which to draw up such a letter, a fact which all the more emphasized how false the accusations had been.

* * * * *

CHAPTER 26

Acts 26:1-32 THE GOSPEL OF PAUL

To understand Paul's defense well, one would have to be as familiar with Jewish thought as was King Agrippa II, since the foundation of Christianity was imbedded in the Scriptures, Jewish customs and beliefs. Paul himself was born a Jew and lived as one; he had even been a Pharisee at one time; everyone knew that. He too lived in expectation of resurrection and of the Messianic era. And the eschatological age had arrived already, realized initially at the Resurrection of Jesus. A faithful Jew should not have thought such a thing impossible, as would have a Gentile who lived in this world without any hope whatever, for Christianity is not merely not opposed to Judaism, but is its perfect fulfillment.

Paul repeated his favorite argument proving his

sincerity—he had been such an ardent follower of the Law that he became one of the most feared persecutors of Christians, pursuing them unceasingly. If he afterwards changed his way of living so suddenly, there must have been some reason. No explanation was possible other than the vision he had had of Jesus on the road to Damascus.

In this marvelous encounter with the Risen Christ, the newly converted Paul was given a command. It is interesting to note how Luke has Christ say the words which in a previous chapter were spoken by Ananias. At any rate, directly or indirectly, it was the Master Who sent Paul. Paul had to become a "martyr"—in other words, a witness of the Resurrection of the Lord. God Himself would protect Paul and save him from the attacks of the Jews and Gentiles, so that he would be able to preach God's call to conversion, to freedom from the snares of Satan and sin and through faith in the Resurrection of Christ, to be incorporated into the inheritance of the saints and the wonderful promises of Scripture concerning the age of salvation.

Paul had affirmed that he had fulfilled this mission towards Jews and Gentiles. Because of it and especially because he had risked his life among the pagans to preach salvation through faith, he had suffered persecution even from some of his own brethren. Paul was careful to note that he had done all of this only because he had received the command from the Lord, and because he was absolutely convinced from his own study of the Scriptures, that the Messiah truly had to suffer, rise, and bring salvation to the Gentiles.

After listening to such a clear presentation of the facts, each one reacted differently, depending on his dispositions. The usually calm Festus reacted as Paul said some would (1 Cor. 1:1 f)—he considered the Gospel folly. Agrippa, on the other hand, was not in any way displeased with Paul's words; he believed in the innocence of the Apostle. At this point Paul had reached the zenith of his preaching mission—he had preached the Word of God to rulers and to kings, and they had vindicated him, even if they had not believed.

* * * * *

CHAPTER 27

Acts 27:1-44 THE HOLY SPIRIT GUIDES PAUL TO ROME

St. Luke was not writing a novel, although this chapter could very well take its place in any travel-book with literary pretentions. Our author intended only to write what was essentially theological in character. From the beginning of the Acts, Luke's central aim was to show how the Gospel through Paul's endeavors came to be transferred from Jerusalem to Rome. Luke intended to show that the salvation rejected by the Sanhedrin was welcome in the center of the pagan world. Providence had used Paul's appeal to Caesar to provide the Apostle with a "free trip" to Rome. It seemed, however, that the elements, which according to ancient superstitions were impregnated with diabolic powers, conspired against the final destination of the

143

Gospel in the Eternal City. According to human foresight the ship and everyone on board should have sunk, but Luke insists that it was the Holy Spirit and not the wind that actually guided the ship. Paul was the one who sailed the crew to Rome, not vice versa. The revelations which the Apostle continued to have during the voyage confirm this.

Theologically, the key to the whole chapter rests in the phrase, "it is necessary," in v.24. In biblical usage this phrase referred to the will of God which so fore-ordained human events, that they would take place in an ordered sequence. In this sense, then, the voyage to Rome, like the one to Jerusalem, was theologically orientated.

v.1. The Augustan cohort—this was most likely an honorary title and not the real name of the cohort.

v.2. Adrumythium—a port of Misia in the Roman province of Asia.

v.2. Aristarchus—cf. Acts 19:29; 20:4; Col. 4:10 ff., 19.

v.9. The Fast—for the feast of Expiation which came in October.

v.14. The northeaster—a raging wind which came from the East-North-East.

v.17. Syrtis—sandbanks off the coast of North Africa near Tunisia, notoriously dangerous because of the sea currents.

v.35. Thanks to God—granted that this phrase is

Eucharistic in its meaning, still Luke probably means a simple breakfast.

v.41. A Shoal—at St. Paul's Bay, Malta, the traditional site of Paul's shipwreck. The description by Luke corresponds to the geographical location.

* * * * *

CHAPTER 28

Acts 28:1-10 THE POWER OF GOD AMIDST THE
BARBARIANS

A Christian divides the world into two categories:
Christians and pagans; a Jew claims that humanity is
composed of Jews and Gentiles; and the Roman-Greeks
distinguished between Greeks and barbarians (cf. Rom.
1:14). Those who did not speak either Greek or Latin
or who were not familiar with Greek culture were
known as "barbarians." The natives of Lystra, whom
we encountered in a previous chapter (14), were certainly considered barbarians; is it not strange that their
reaction to Paul's miracle was very similar to that of the
Maltese? Luke has consistently emphasized that the
salvation which the Jews rejected was then offered not
only to the Gentiles, but even to barbarians, and though
both were content to eat of the crumbs from the table,
the honored guests were reluctant to dine and feast.

147

Luke does not say that Paul preached the Gospel in Malta, yet it is hardly conceivable that after so many miracles he could have passed by such an opportunity to plant the Gospel in the hearts of natives so well disposed.

v.1. Malta—an island which was first colonized by the Phoenicians, but afterwards, during the Punic Wars, passed into the hands of the Romans. Punic was still spoken there in the first century after Christ.

v.3. A Viper—presently there are no poisonous snakes in Malta; this should not be very surprising if one would recall that in such a small and densely inhabited island poisonous reptiles are very likely to become extinct.

v.7. In the Neighborhood—recently in Malta a Roman Villa at Bur Murrad, close to the Bay of St. Paul, was discovered, dating back to the first century. A rock was also discovered in the ruins which bore the engraving of a *fish*.

v.7. Publius—this title of the head man of the island has been proven from Greek and Latin inscriptions.

Acts 28:11-16 O ROMA NOBILIS!

Rome draws near. Paul is joyously received by the Christians of both Puteoli and the Eternal City who had come to know him through his famous letter written to them. At last he had entered the Capital of the ancient world—his dream is finally realized. It would be wrong to say that the Gospel reached Rome simultaneously with Paul, since some of the Jewish communities had already been evangelized by other bearers of the Gospel, notably among them St. Peter himself. But in the Acts, which follows a unique historical outline, it is the Apostle of the Gentiles who overcomes the limitations demanded by Jewish Law, and it is he who diffuses the Word of God among the Gentiles, an achievement which will soon bear much fruit.

Paul remained a prisoner in Rome for two years. The reader will probably be very curious to know what happened afterwards, what the outcome of the decision before Caesar was. Did Paul suffer martyrdom?—Luke abruptly finishes the narration after having accomplished what he set out to do, namely, to show how the Gospel which was rejected in Jerusalem became accepted in Rome. Paul's trial probably came to nought, since his accusers apparently never did present their charges in court within the period of time prescribed by Roman Law. The beheading of Paul not only does not form part of the plan of the Acts, but it would in fact have destroyed everything that Luke had taken pains to prove all along—that Paul was found innocent before each and every one of the legal tribunals. In the scheme of the Acts, the account of Paul's condemnation would not have been a victory, but rather a total calamity; hence it was very wise to discontinue the narrative at this point. We know from various other sources that Paul made many journeys from Rome into Asia and possibly even into Spain. He suffered martydom under Nero in 67 A.D.

v.11. The Twin Brothers—Castor and Pollux, the gods of sailors.
v.13. Puteoli—the port used for sea commerce with the Orient. There were many Jews who lived there, among whom were to be found converts to Christianity.
v.15. Forum of Appius and Three Taverns—two stops 43 and 33 miles along the Appian Way respectively.
v.16. A soldier that guarded him—a prisoner in loose custody was kept under surveillance by one guard.

Acts 28:17-31 "YOU SHALL INDEED HEAR BUT WILL NOT UNDERSTAND"

Having arrived at Rome, Paul presented himself to the elders of the Hebrew community, before whom he declared himself innocent, charging the Jews in Jerusalem with "having delivered me into the hands of the Romans." He preached the Gospel to them, but with less success than he had had with Jews of other regions. As a result, Paul, in the name of the Holy Spirit, passed sentence on the obdurate Jews, thus crowning Luke's main thesis.

The author of the Acts intended the two verses of Isaiah in the sense rendered by the Septuagint translation. Isaiah described the blindness of the Jews who saw with their own eyes and heard with their own ears the salvation promised by God to Israel, but because they were not properly disposed, they did not understand. Because they had never entered into the spirit of divine revelation and because they had never observed the law as they should have, their hearts became hardened. The call to faith and conversion found them weak and unprepared. Subconsiously they had been afraid of a true conversion and because of this they would continue to walk with the veil over their eyes.

Since the Gentiles were better disposed, possessing a thirst for Justice which they could not satisfy except by drinking of the Gospel, the Word of God passed over to them. The Jews became infuriated, but God used this jealousy too for His own salvific designs (Rom. 9-11). After the conversion of the Gentiles, the veil which had covered the eyes of the Jews would fall away and they too, able to answer the call of the Holy Spirit with their faith, would finally be converted to the Lord (2 Cor. 3:7-18; Acts 3:20).

v.19. Though I had no charge to bring against my nation—among the Jews, as among the Christians, it was disdainful to accuse co-religionists in any pagan tribunal (1 Cor. 6:1-6).

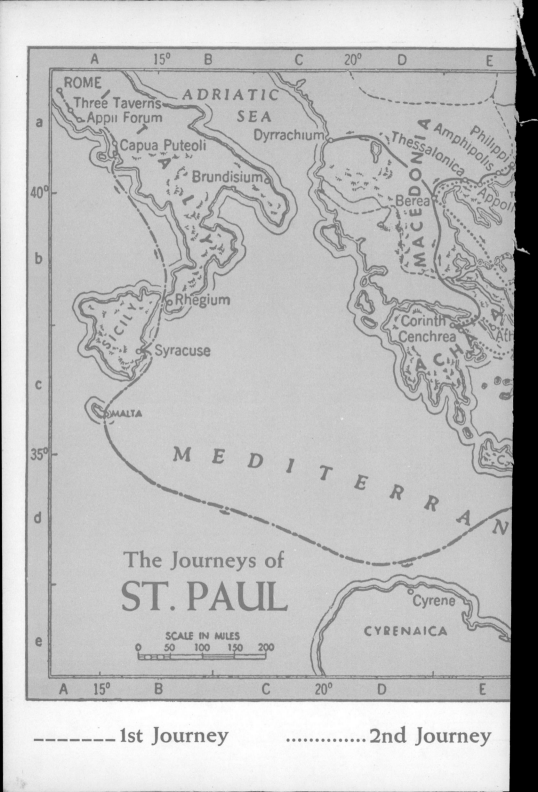

The Journeys of
ST. PAUL

SCALE IN MILES
0   50   100   150   200

———— 1st Journey   .... 2nd Journey